Guide
To
Fingerprint Identification
And
Classification

Understanding Fingerprint Patterns and the Henry Classification System

Monika Reinhardt

Second Edition

This book was written to give the reader and/or student an easier understanding about Fingerprint Identification and Classification. It is designed as a guide and reference tool.

This guide is a collection of Fingerprint Identification and Classification information, notes, and material from several different sources; i.e. Lectures, Courses, Seminars, and the FBI's "Science of Fingerprints."

Monika@OnlineBusinessEducation.com
OnlineBusinessEducation.com

ISBN-13: 978-069273155-0 (Online Business Education)
ISBN-10: 0692731555

Second Edition

First Printing 2004

Dedication

I dedicated this book to my mother, **Ursela Buge**, whom I thank for being there for me with her love, support, encouragement and friendship; as well as believing in me to make it when I immigrated to the United States.

To my brother **Ralf "Ralli" Rehder** (1961-1984), who was taken from us way to young!

To **Diana Castro**, Los Angeles Police Department, Principal Forensic Print Specialist, Latent Print Division (Retired); and Instructor for Fingerprint Classification at East Los Angeles College for her support, for being my mentor, for being a great instructor and most of all for being my best friend.

Acknowledgements

My biggest Thank You goes to **Diana Castro**. She shared her knowledge and experience with me. Without her teaching I could not have completed this book to the stage it is now. Her motivation and encouragement has helped me to bring out the best of my abilities and talents.

I also want to thank **Dr. Janis Cavanaugh** for creating the Forensic Program and giving students and professionals an opportunity to learn about a very important part of law enforcement.

A big Thank You goes to **Fresno City College** for using this book for their Fingerprint Course.

I want to thank **Ron Smith**, of Ron Smith & Associates, for demystifying palm prints for me and other students. The way he presented his course "Demystifying Palm Prints" he created an enjoyable learning environment, which in turn helped me to understand the complex topic of palm print identification.

I thank the **Federal Bureau of Investigation (F.B.I.)** for publishing the Book "The Science of Fingerprints." This book was used through my first course on fingerprints, which lead to my notes collection and this guide.

Foreword

I started this guide with my notes during the Fall 1999 Semester while I studied Fingerprint Classification and Identification at East Los Angeles College. Once I organized my notes typing them out and putting them into a binder it started to become a reference guide. Bringing my organized notes to class sparked curiosity and interest from other students, especially the ones struggling to keep up due to "Fingerprint Classification Confusion." My notes helped them to get a better understanding of this tough subject and helped a few to pass the class.

During the Summer and Fall Semesters of 2000, I went through a Forensic Identification course and updated the Guide as I learned more about Fingerprint Classification and Identification.

I became a Crime Scene Investigator and a Police Officer. Throughout my career I was able to apply my skills and knowledge of fingerprints in law enforcement and crime scene investigations. It allowed me to know how to find, collect, and process fingerprint evidence, solve cases, and testify as an expert.

Table Of Contents

Chapter   Page

Chapter 1 – **Introduction**

Personal identification of individuals occupied legitimately, and/or criminals wishing to escape detection, has long been one of humankind's most profound concerns. Since early in history man has used various identifiers, such as tribal symbols, crowns, scepters, flags, marks, and the cross, as means of recognition. With the advent of modern society came a pressing need for more personal and positive methods of identification. Thus, the stage was set for the first observations of fingerprints, and the beginnings of a science, which was to become the bulwark of identification.

A fingerprint is an impression or reproduction of the friction skin on a surface.

The fingerprint science is founded on the science of anatomy, biology, embryology, genetics and neurology. Hence it has been referred to as "an applied science".

The scientific study of fingerprints for the purpose of identification is called Dactyloscopy.

The science of fingerprints is based on two facts – they are permanent and unique. No two persons have the same fingerprints.

The Fingerprint Expert gives much consideration to the Galton Details of each fingerprint he/she examines before giving any testimony regarding the comparison of an inked print and a patent print.

History

The history of fingerprints lets us know that early civilizations were aware of the designs on their fingers.

The historic events in fingerprinting concerning dates and happenings have no real affect on the classification of fingerprints, but the events themselves are informative facts in the field of fingerprints.

China is credited with the first use of fingerprints as early as the 11th century. The ancient Chinese placed thumbprints in the city seals used on legal documents. This procedure was believed to keep solemnity to legal transactions. It is not known if the Chinese to had any possible knowledge of the value of fingerprints for personal identification.

Below are some important historical milestones of identification. Associated with the historical developments are the names of pioneers in the field, all of whom contributed in his own way to the evolution of an effective fingerprint identification system as the one presently used by The Federal Bureau of Identification.

Historical References:

- **Prehistoric Indians** in Nova Scotia drew pictures of hands with ridge patterns on cliffs. Circular edgings on the fingertips are representative of friction ridge patterns and on the thumb a spiral whorl had been carved. This carving is considered to be at least several hundred years old and it is believed to be **the first documented**

anthropological illustration depicting the friction ridges and flexion creases of the hand.

- Fingerprint impressions were found on clay pottery, clay tablets, scrolls, etc. **200 B.C. in Babylon**. The people probably used fingerprints to seal business transactions and to identify the author of a specific manuscript.

- The **Rule of Hammurabi from 1792 to 1750 BC** indicates that law officers were authorized to secure the fingerprints of arrested persons.

- Fingerprints were found on 3,000 year old **King Tut's Tomb**

- Recently, in **China**, fingerprints were found on earthenware over 6,000 years old. These are to be considered to be the oldest found to date.

- The **first written reference** to using fingerprints as a means to identify people was by the **Chinese in 650 AD**.

- In 1684 **Dr. Nehemiah Grew** published a paper of the observations he made in London describing the ridges and pores found on the hands and feet.

- In 1686 **Marcello Malpighi** was the first to use the microscope to note "elevated ridges" on the palmar surface, which were "drawn out into loops and spirals".

- **Johannes Evangelist Purkinje** published a thesis in 1823 commenting on the diversity of ridge patterns and put these patterns into nine varieties.

- **Sir William Herschel** was the first to recognize the value of fingerprints and to use them for identification. He was an administrator in India and in 1858 he observed the Indian people using fingerprints as signatures on documents and contracts. In 1860 he expanded the use of fingerprints to various types of fraud. In 1877 he controlled the courts, prisons, registration of deeds, and payment of government pensions. He wrote the Hooghly Letter, which described ideas and suggested that the use of fingerprints be expanded and used in other areas.

- **Dr. Henry Faulds** studied fingerprints and mentioned to Charles Darwin that fingerprints can be classified easily and ridge detail is unique. He mentioned that friction ridges never change. He was the first to publish his information in 1880 to connect on the use of fingerprints to solve crimes, and catch and apprehend criminals by locating fingerprints at crime scenes.

- In 1882 **Gilbert Thompson** of the U.S. Geological Survey Team used his own fingerprint on Commissary orders to prevent forgery.

- In 1883 **Mark Twain** made reference to a murderer being identified by his thumbprint in the book "Life On The Mississippi."

- In 1893 **Mark Twain** again used the Fingerprint Identification Technique in the book "Pudd'n Head Wilson" to identify a criminal in court.

- **Sir Francis Galton** was an anthropologist who encountered a letter from Faulds that was written to his cousin Darwin. In 1892 he published a book called "Fingerprints". In 1893 he suggested that fingerprints be added to Scotland Yard's files. The Galton Details were named after him.

- In 1892 **Juan Vucetich** from Argentina experiments with fingerprints and worked out his own classification system, but his superiors did not allow him to use fingerprints. Vucetich's theory was proven when the Rojas Murders were solved with fingerprints. That was also the first murder solved with fingerprints.

- **Sir Edward Henry**, also in India, began to correspond with **Galton** and developed the Henry Classification. The Henry classification had all fingerprints typed. There are 1,024 primary classifications with secondary breakdowns within these classifications. He wrote a book "Classification and Uses of Fingerprints." In 1901 he was the Assistant Commissioner of Police in charge of Criminal Identification a New Scotland Yard. Anthropometry was slowly being phased out. Even though the classification system was named after him, Hague and Bose, who worked with Henry, revised it. He never took credit for the system, but the fact that the Henry System is the basis for most of the present day classification system speaks for itself.

- In 1902 the New York Civil Service System used fingerprints to prevent fraud in Civil Service Testing.

- In 1903 Sing Sing Prison claimed the first Criminal Identification System.

- In 1904 Leavenworth Federal Prison and the Saint Louis Police Department established Fingerprint Bureaus.

- In 1905 the **U.S. Army** adopted the Fingerprint System as a means of positive Identification. The **U.S. Navy** adopted the system in 1907 the, and the **U.S. Marines** in 1908.

- In 1924 an Act of Congress established the Identification Division of the F.B.I. The original file had a total of 810,000 fingerprint cards.

These where events and people that the shaped the future and advancement of fingerprint identification. The people of vision who applied the science as they knew it and due to their unselfish efforts fingerprint identification has become what it is today – the most positive method of personal identification.

Chapter 2 - Fingerprint Identification

Pattern Types

Fingerprints may be resolved intó three basic pattern types:

1. **Arch**
2. **Loop**
3. **Whorl**

Only 5% of the population has Arch Patterns. 30% of the population has Whorl Patterns, and 65% of the population has Loop Patterns.

The patterns may be further divided into sub-groups by means of the smaller differences existing between the patterns in the same general group.

1. **Arch**
   a.) Plain Arch
   b.) Tented Arch

2. **Loop**
   a.) Radial Loop
   b.) Ulnar Loop

3. **Whorl**
   a.) Plain Whorl
   b.) Central Pocket Loop Whorl
   c.) Double Loop Whorl
   d.) Accidental Whorl

Any of these eight pattern types can appear in any finger, or all ten fingers can have the same patterns. Some pattern types appear more often than others. Ten tented arches, ten radial loops, or ten accidental patterns are very rare. Some pattern types appear more often than others. Because nothing is consistent with the frequency of pattern appearance, the number of possible pattern combinations is large. This number of pattern combinations makes it necessary to separate similar pattern combinations into groups. This grouping, and the information from each pattern type gathered, result in the classification formula.

Pattern Area

The pattern area is the part of a loop or whorl in which the cores, deltas, and ridges appear.

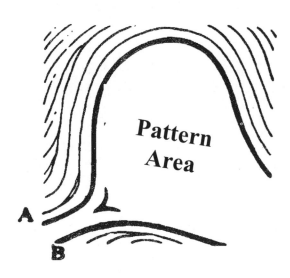

The Pattern Area includes only those ridges within the type lines. Nothing outside the type lines is considered in fingerprint classification.

Type Lines

Type lines are the two innermost ridges that start parallel, diverge, and surround, or tend to surround the pattern area.

Type Lines . . .
"A" and "B" are the type lines of this loop pattern print. Type lines are no thicker than other ridge lines.

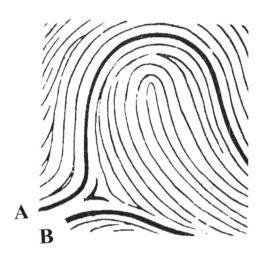

All fingerprints have several that enter on one side of the finger and start to travel across the finger. The type line definition specifically refers to two ridges running parallel. After they diverge the ridge may end abruptly. When the type line ends after the divergence the next ridge to the outside is used.

Type lines can have several shapes. There is no specific requirement for the length of type lines, but they must run parallel for a distance to be considered type lines.

A formation where an angle is present cannot be used as a type line.

Type lines may be very short . . . As in the print below. Here the outer type line "A" is broken, but it nevertheless forms the basis for the surrounding pattern. "B" is the inner type line of the pattern. Both "A" and "B" eventually become parallel.

Angles are never formed by a single ridge...
They are formed by one ridge abutting another. Therefore, an angular formation cannot be a type line. In this illustration "A" and "B" join at an angle. Ridge "B" does not run parallel with ridge "D", and ridge "A" does not diverge. The correct type lines are "C" and "D".

A

A

The Ridges Marked "A" and "A"

Are not considered type lines. In this case the lines do not run parallel, therefore, do not meet the requirements of being type lines. The correct type lines are those marked "T" and "T".

Type Lines are not always two continuous; they are more often found to be broken. When there is a definite break in a type line, the ridge immediately *outside* of it is considered as its continuation.

Within these type lines is found the entire pattern area of the fingerprint.

The pattern area includes only those ridges within the type lines. Nothing outside the type lines is considered in fingerprint classification.

To locate type lines on a fingerprint, look for the ridges embracing the loops or whorls in the pattern area. These ridges just above, below or to the outside of the patterns are the type lines.

Type lines are not always continuous ridges. Frequently, they are broken lines. In making a ridge tracing, should you find a definite break in a type line, look for a ridge immediately outside. This is considered to be the continuation of the previous type line.

Type lines are no thicker than other ridges.

Sometimes type lines may be very short. Care must be exercised in their location.

When locating type lines it is necessary to keep in mind the distinction between a divergence and a bifurcation.

Bifurcation: the forking or dividing of one line into two or more branches. There is no limit to the numbers of branches being present, but it is rare that there are more than four. An angle is formed ate the exact point where the ridge splits, or becomes more than one.

The amount of pressure applied when rolling the print can have an effect of the appearance of a bifurcation.

Too much pressure can cause an ending ridge become a bifurcation.

A bifurcation must have a short length of the ridges before the bifurcation. When the short length of the ridge is not present the shape is called a meeting of two ridges.

Divergence: the spreading apart of two lines which has been running parallel or nearly parallel.

A single ridge may bifurcate, but may not be said to diverge. The two forks of a bifurcation may never constitute type lines. The only exception is when forks run parallel after bifurcating and then diverge.

Angles are never formed by a single ridge but by the abutting of one ridge against another.

The point of a divergence is at the exact point where it is obvious the two ridges are starting to spread evenly.

Focal points: within the pattern areas of loops and whorls are enclosed the **focal points**, which are used to classify them. These points are called **delta** and **core**.

Delta

The delta is the point on a ridge at or in front of and nearest the center of the divergence of the type lines; Is the innermost point on the first ridge obstruction of any type, which is directly in front of, or nearest the point where the two type lines diverge.

The delta is the starting point for the ridge count of the pattern.

The delta might be a dot, or a short ridge, the forking point of a ridge that becomes divided (this is called a bifurcation), the ending of a ridge or simply that point on the first recurring ridge in the pattern which is centered nearest the point where the type lines diverge.

The delta must be within the type lines to be considered a part of a fingerprint pattern.

13

Deltas may be found in loop or whorl patterns, but not in arch patterns.

The Delta may be:
- A bifurcation
- An abrupt ending ridge
- A dot
- A short ridge
- A meeting of two ridges
- A point on the first recurving ridge located nearest to the center and in front of the divergence of the type lines

There is a similarity between the use of the word "delta" in physical geography and fingerprints. The island formed in front of the diverging sides if the banks where the stream empties at its mouth corresponds to the delta in fingerprints. This is the first obstruction of any at the point of divergence of the type lines in front of or nearest the center of the divergence.

A delta can be located on either side of en ending ridge, depending on where the end is located – in front of behind the point of divergence.

When there is a choice between two or more possible deltas, the following rules govern:

- The delta may not be located at a bifurcation, which does not open toward the core.

- When there is a choice between a bifurcation and another type of delta, equally close to the point of divergence, the bifurcation is selected.

- When there is a series of bifurcations opening toward the core at the point of divergence of the two type lines, the bifurcation nearest the core is chosen as the delta.

- The delta may not be located in the middle of a ridge running between the type lines toward the core, but the nearer end only.

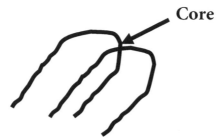

Core

If the ridge is entirely with in the pattern area, the delta is located at the end nearer the point of divergence of the type lines.

If the ridge enters the pattern area from a point below the divergence of the type lines, however, the delta must be located at the end nearer the core.

The delta is the point from which to start the ridge counting. In the loop type pattern the ridges intervening between the delta and the core are counted.

Core

The core is the center of a pattern area and located on or within what is referred as the "innermost sufficient recurve" of a loop.

It is usually a visible part of the pattern, such as a dot or the ending of a center ridge or rod.

When it is not, the position of the core is calculated according to specific guidelines. The shapes found inside the innermost looping ridge will be normally be a length of a ridge. These length are called either a rods or spikes. A rod or spike must be as high as the shoulder before it can be considered as a core.

In this way a core position may sometimes even be assigned to an arch pattern, which never has a core.

When the innermost sufficient recurve contains no ending ridge or rod rising as high as the shoulders of a loop (that point at which the curve begins) the core is placed on the shoulder of the loop which is farther from the delta.

When the shoulders are equidistant to the delta, the core is considered to be at the center of the sufficient recurve.

When the innermost sufficient recurve contains an uneven number of rods rising as high as the shoulders, the core is at the end of the center rod.

When the innermost sufficient recurve contains an even number of rods rising as high as the shoulders, the core is at the end of the one of the two center rods which is farther from the delta, the two center rods being treated as though they where connected by a recurving ridge.

The core is the second of the two focal points.

The core is the approximate center of the finger impression.

The following rules govern the selection of the core of the loop:

- The core is placed upon or within the innermost sufficient recurve.

- When the innermost re-curve contains no ending ridge or rod rising as high as the shoulders of the loop, the core is placed on the shoulders of the loop farther from the delta. The exception to this rule is when both shoulders are equidistant to the delta; the core is located on the center of the sufficient recurve.

- When the innermost sufficient recurve contains an uneven number of rods rising as high as the shoulders, the core is placed upon the end of the center rod whether it touches the looping ridge or not.

- When the innermost sufficient recurve contains an even number of rods rising as high as the shoulders, the core is placed upon the end of the farther one of the two center rods being treated as though they where connected by a re-curving ridge.

- When the innermost sufficient recurve contains an uneven number of rods rising as high as the shoulders, the core is placed upon the end of the center rod whether it touches the looping ridge or not.

- When the innermost sufficient recurve contains an even number of rods rising as high as the shoulders, the core is placed upon the end of the farther one of the two center rods being treated as though they where connected by a re-curving ridge.

The shoulders of a loop are the points at which the recurving ridge definitely turns inward or curves.

When The Core Is Located On A Spike . . .

Which touches the inside of the innermost recurving ridge, the recurve is included in the ridge count only when the delta is located below a line drawn at right angles to the spike. Examples of this rule are shown below. If the delta is located in areas "A" the recurving ridge is counted. If the delta is in areas "B", the recurving ridge is not counted.

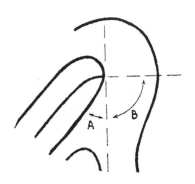 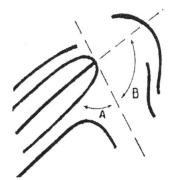

Applications of Deltas and Cores

Both the delta and the core within the pattern area are of special interest to the fingerprint examiner. They serve as important points of reference in more detailed examination of latent prints.

Both the delta and the core are two focal points that are of particular importance in fingerprint classification. An incorrect choice of either of these points can make a difference of several ridge counts, or the incorrect trace of a whorl.

For example, to be classified as a whorl, a pattern must have two deltas, one at each side of the pattern, within the type lines.

To determine whether a pattern is a plain whorl or a central pocket loop, an imaginary line is drawn from one delta to the other.

If the line touches any of the circular-type ridges, the pattern is a plain whorl.

If the line does not touch such a ridge, the pattern is a central pocket loop.

The rule is that a recurve must have no appendage abutting upon it at a right angle between the shoulders and on the outside. If such an appendage is present between the shoulders of a loop, that loop is considered spoiled and the next loop outside will be considered to locate the core.

If there are two loops side by side at the center, the two loops are considered as one. When the shoulder line is found to cross exactly at the point of intersection of the two loops the two loops are considered one.

Rods: Straight ridges, most commonly, they are enclosed by the innermost recurve of a loop pattern.

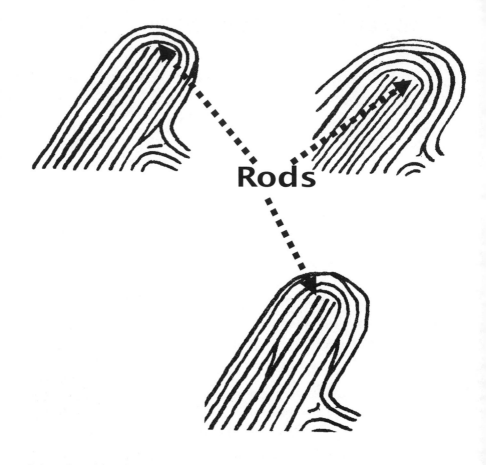

Rods

If the shoulder line is above the point of intersection of the two loops, the two are considered as one with two rods.

If the shoulder line is below the point of intersection of the loops, again the two are treated as one with two rods.

A white space must intervene between the delta and the first ridge count. If no such interval exists, the first ridge must be disregarded.

Rods or spikes that touch the inside of a looping ridge but do not go through it do not spoil it. They are as high as the shoulders and are considered the core.

Delta and Core Samples

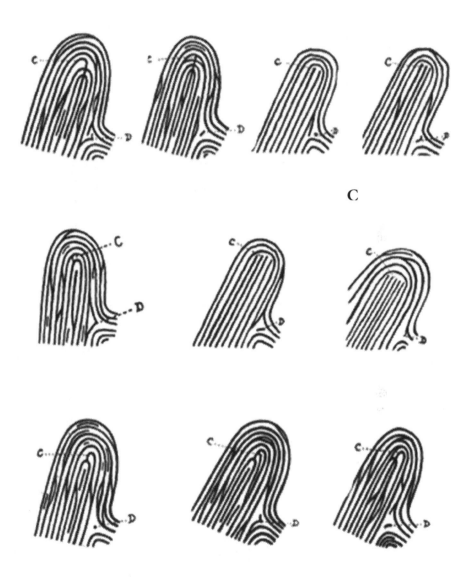

C

Chapter 3 – Ridges And Details

Friction Ridges

The friction ridges which form pattern types never change in appearance, except for size and accidental or intentional scarring. The friction ridges are present on our fingers before birth and are one of the last things to disappear from the fingers after death. Since the ridges never change, the classification of fingerprints never changes. A classification obtained today should be the same twenty years later, unless there has been a deliberate attempt to alter the fingerprint pattern, which is rarely successful and extremely painful, or an injury or amputation has occurred. An amputation or scarring can cause a different classification result.

Ridge Counting

The number of ridges intervening between the delta and the core is known as the ridge count.

Ridge count is defined as the number of ridges touched or crossed by an imaginary line between the delta and the core.

Many Different Types of Ridges . . .

May be included in the ridge count, as long as they are true ridges, of the same thickness as other ridges and cross or touch the imaginary line between the delta and core. On which the count is made. If a bifurcation of a ridge occurs exactly at the point where the imaginary line would be drawn, two ridges are counted. Where the line crosses an island, both sides are counted. Fragments and dots are counted as ridges only if they appear to be as thick and heavy as the other ridges in the immediate pattern.

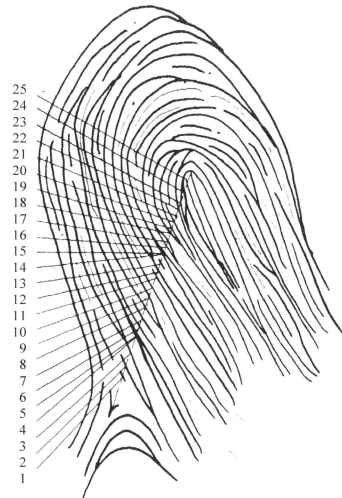

1. Short Ridge
2. Bifurcation
3. Bifurcation
4. Bifurcation
5. Bifurcation
6. Ridge
7. Ending Ridge
8. Bifurcation
9. Bifurcation
10. Ridge
11. Ending Ridge
12. Ridge
13. Short Ridge
14. Bifurcation
15. Bifurcation
16. Island
17. Island
18. Bifurcation
19. Bifurcation
20. Ending Ridge
21. Dot
22. Ridge
23. Island
24. Island
25. Ending Ridge

Each ridge, which *crosses or touches* an imaginary line drawn from the delta to the core, is counted.

Neither delta nor core is counted.

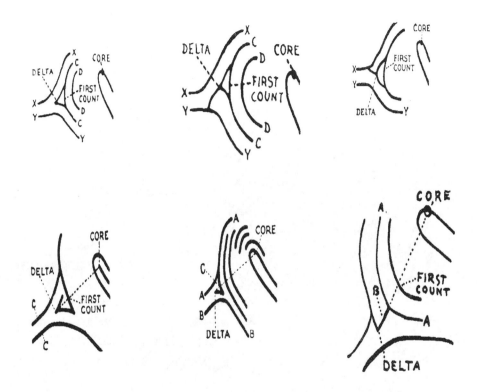

Ridge Counts Are Made . . .

- across an imaginary line from the delta to the core.
- the delta and the core are not included in the ridge count.

Incipient ridges are those ridges that for some unknown reason stopped growing before they reached their full size. Some lighter or thinner ridge lines are caused by the splitting or fraying of the ridges. Sometimes ingrained dirt will cause a similar condition between the ridges. Incipient ridges and lighter ridges are not considered ridges and should not be counted.

When the core is located on a spike which touches the inside of the innermost re-curving ridge, the recurve is included in the ridge count only when the delta is located below a line drawn at right angles to the spike.

Many different types of ridges may be included in the ridge count, as long as they are true ridges, of the same thickness as other ridges and cross or touch an imaginary line between the delta and the core on which the count is made.

If a bifurcation of a ridge occurs exactly at the point where the imaginary line would be drawn, two ridges are counted.

Island

An **Island** is a single ridge, which forks into two and rejoins into one ridge again. The island is also known as an **Enclosure**.

Where the line crosses an island, both sides are counted.

Fragments and dots are counted as ridges only if they appear to be as thick and heavy as the other ridges in the immediate pattern. Variations in inking and the pressure must, of course, be considered.

The Henry-Galton system further utilizes the delta and the core, together, in counting the friction ridges in a pattern.

The delta is considered the outer terminus and the core is considered the inner terminus; counting the ridges that intersect this line provides a figure, which is an additional identifying factor of the print being examined.

When the delta is not visible, the location of the delta is anticipated. The visible ridges are counted from the core to the anticipated location of the delta and a "+" sign is added to the ridge count number (10+ for example).

Galton Details

Once you have located the pattern area, type lines, core, and delta(s), you must examine the structure of the ridge within this pattern area for further distinguishing features, such as appendages, diverging ridges, bifurcations, dots, islands, short ridges, enclosures and ridge endings.

Here is what the Galton Details look like:

Converging Ridges

Two or more ridges meet. The meeting point is called the "point of convergence".

Diverging Ridges

Two ridges run parallel, or nearly parallel, for some distance, then swing away from each other.

Appendage

A ridge which abuts another ridge. You will find it frequently where a recurve makes its turn.

Bifurcation

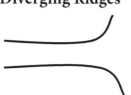

A ridge, which diverges or forks to form to two or more ridges. Sometimes known as a bifurcating ridge.

Rods

These are straight ridges. Most commonly, they are enclosed by the innermost recurve of the loop pattern.

Dot

Round or oval in shape, the dot is sometimes referred to as an island. It may be considered a short ridge if it contains even one pore.

Ridge Ending

This is the ending point of a ridge.

Incipient Ridge

This is not a true ridge. Fragments of loose skin or other debris located between well-defined ridges may appear as a faint ridge on a print. Such marks are never used in classifying or comparison.

Island

A single ridge, which forks into two and rejoins into one ridge again. Also known as an Enclosure.

To determine whether a faint ridgeline is a true ridgeline or an incipient ridgeline, compare its width to that of other ridges within the same pattern area. If it is not the same width, it is to be considered an incipient ridge.

Chapter 4 -
Loop and Arch Pattern Types

The Loop

The loop pattern is the most common of the eight pattern types. 65% of all fingerprints are believed to be loop patterns.

Loop patterns have ridges, which move in one direction and then recurve, to return to the direction from which they started.

To qualify as a loop pattern a print must have one ore more ridges that meet this description.

There cannot be a loop unless there is a recurve or turning back on itself of one or more of the ridges. The sufficient recurve is the area between the shoulders on the outside of the looping ridge. Other conditions have to be considered, like a pattern must possess several requisites before it may be properly classified as a loop. The sufficient recurve must be free of appendages at right angles at any point between the shoulders.

A loop may begin from either from the left side of a finger or from the right of a finger.

If a loop opens in the direction of the little finger, it is called an ulnar loop.

If a loop opens in the direction of the thumb, it is called a radial loop.

When a recurve is spoiled it is necessary to go to the next recurving ridge to the outside

The outside bone in the arm is called the Ulna Bone, and the inside bone of the arm is called the Radial Bone.

Loop patterns that have looping ridges coming in on the little finger side of either hand and going out on the little finger side are called Ulnar Loops.

Loop patterns that have looping ridges coming in on the thumb side and going out on the thumb side of either hand are called Radial Loops. The Ulnar and Radial loops are very similar in appearance, with direction being the only difference, but they have the same requirements causing them to be called loops.

Ulnar loops and radial loops are classified according to the way they appear on the hand, not on the print card. Because of the reverse sequence of prints of the left hand fingers on the fingerprint card, a radial loop on the index finger of the left hand, for example, would appear to be an ulnar loop based on the fact that it opens toward the square containing the little finger.

A loop is the that type of fingerprint pattern in which one or more of the ridges enter on either side of the impression, recurve, touch or pass an imaginary line drawn from the delta to the core, and terminate or tend to terminate on or toward the same side of the impression from whence such ridge or ridges.

Essentials of a Loop

- A sufficient recurve
- A delta
- A ridge count across a looping ridge

A **sufficient recurve** may be defined as that part of a recurving ridge between the shoulders of a loop. It must be free of any appendages abutting upon the outside of the re-curve at a right angle.

Sufficient has more than one meaning. It means good, or not spoiled, or enough. After a looping ridge has made its 180 degree turn it must continue far enough to touch or cross an imaginary line from the delta to the farthest shoulder, the core.

Appendages - much care must be exercised in interpreting appendages, because they sometimes change the shape of the re-curving ridge to which they are connected. For example, a loop with an appendage abutting upon its re-curve between the shoulders and at right angles will appear sometimes with the re-curve totally destroyed.

An appendage must be at right angles to the recurve area. An appendage, which is less than right angles, is considered to flow off smoothly and not spoil the recurve.

An appendage must have enough length to show a flat side as opposed to a round look.

An appendage which spoils a recurve and is as high as the shoulders to the next recurve will become the core even if it touches the recurve. As long as the appendage does not go through the recurve it does not spoil.

The same rule applies to a whorl re-curve.

The proper location of the core and delta is of extreme importance, for an error in the location of either might cause this pattern to be classified as a loop.

Radial and Ulnar Loops

The terms "Ulnar" and "Radial" are derived from the radius and the ulnar bones of the forearm.

Loops, which flow the direction of the ulnar bone (toward the little finger), are called ulnar loops and those, which flow in the direction of the radius bone (toward the thumb), are called radial loops.

If a loop's opening is in the direction of the little finger, it is called an ulnar loop.

If a loop opens in the direction of the thumb, it is called a radial loop.

Ulnar loops and radial loops are classified according to the way they appear on the hand, not on the print card.

Note that the ulnar and radial loops are also called slanted loops. If the ridge flow of an impression opens to the left it is called a left slanted loop. If the ridge flow of an impression opens to the right it is called a right slanted loop.

Loop Pattern Samples

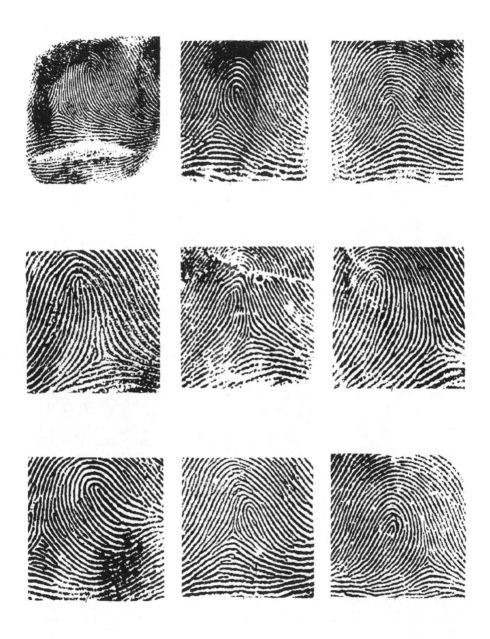

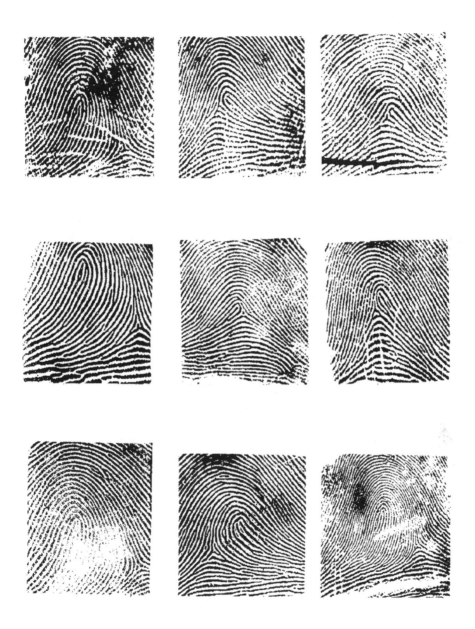

The Plain Arch

The plain arch can best described as *a fingerprint where the ridges enter on one side of the finger, move across the finger with a slight rise or wave in the center, and exit on the opposite side.*

Only 5% of fingerprint files are either plain arches or tented arches.

The ridges literally form an arch pattern as they move from one side of the print to the other. They do not recurve.

The ridges in the plain arch rise gradually upward and are rounded at the top in the center of the print.

There may be various ridge formations such as ending ridges, bifurcations, dots and islands involved in this type of pattern, but they all tend to follow the general ridge contour as mentioned above.

A plain arch approximating a tented arch, as the rising ridge cannot be considered an *upthrust* because it is a continuous and *not an ending ridge.*

Plain Arch Pattern Samples

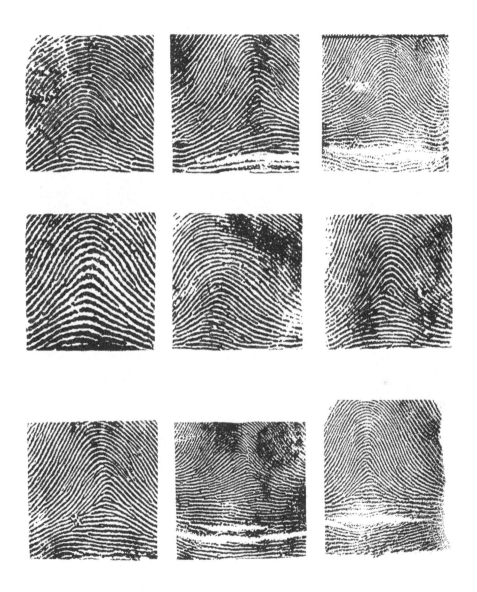

The ridges in the plain arch rise gradually upward and are rounded at the top in the center of the print.

Tented Arch

In the tented arch most of the ridges enter upon one side of the impression and flow or tend to flow out upon the other side, as in the plain arch pattern, however, the ridge or ridges at the center do not. This type is more sharply upthrust, sometimes almost spiky.

Upthrust - An ending ridge of any length rising at a sufficient degree   from the horizontal plane, i.e., 45° or more.

There are three types of tented arches. The classification formula does not identify the type of tented arch, only the pattern.

- The **Angle** type where ridges at the center form a definite angle (i.e., 90° or less). The ridge will end in an upward direction somewhere near the center of the print. At the same time another ridge might be coming from the other side and end in an upward direction near the center meeting the first ridge forming an angle. The angle must be sharp, a formation that is smooth over the top is considered a plain arch.

- The **Upthrust** type where one or more ridges at the center form an upthrust. When there is no second ridge present to form an angle and the ridge ends upward, the pattern is called a tented arch if the upthrust is 45° or more. A level plane must be established in order to decide the 45°. When a finger is inked and rolled on a fingerprint card there is an area under the pattern area where the ink did not touch the card, called the flexure area or the place where the finger makes its first bend. By using the flexure area as a level plane it will be much easier to make the 45° decision.

- The **Loop Type Tented Arch** has two of the basic or essential characteristics of the loop, but lacking the third. For example if a pattern has a delta and a core, but lacks a ridge count it is considered a loop type tented arch. It should be remembered that the mere converging of two ridges does not form a recurve, without which there can be no loop.

There are many patterns which at first sight resemble tented arches but which on close inspection are found to be loops, as where one looping ridge will be found in almost vertical position within the pattern area, entirely free from and passing in front of the delta.

It must be remembered that a recurve must be free of any appendage abutting upon it at right angle between the shoulders, and true ridge count is obtained by crossing a looping ridge freely, with a white space intervening between the delta and the core.

There are tented arches having loop formations within the pattern area but with deltas upon the loops, by reason of which it is impossible to secure a ridge count.

Some tented arches have two of the loop characteristics, a recurve and a delta, but lack the third - the ridges count.

Some patterns have spaces between the type lines at their divergence and show nothing, which could be considered as delta formations, except the looping ridges. Such patterns are classified as tented arches because the ridge count necessary for a loop is lacking.

When interpreting a pattern consisting of two ending ridges and a delta, but lacking a recurve, *do not* confuse the ridge count of the tented arch with that of the ridge count of a loop.

The ridge count of a tented arch is merely a convention of fingerprinting; a fiction designed to facilitate a scientific classification of tented arches, and had no connection with a loop.

The ridge count referred to in connection with the tented arches possessing ending ridges and no ridge count ids obtained by imagining that the ending ridge are joined by a recurve only for the purpose of locating the core and obtaining a ridge count. If this point is secure in the mind of the classifier, little difficulty will be encountered.

- **Angles** formed by the abutting ridges in the center of the pattern are *tented arch* pattern.

- The presence of the slightest upthrust at the center of the impression is enough to classify a pattern as a *tented arch*.

- If an upthrust is not an ending ridge, no angle being present, the pattern is classified as a *plain arch*.

- The presence of a sufficient rise could always be ascertained because of the space intervening between the ending ridge and the ridge immediately beneath it, so that it is safe to classify such patterns as *tented arches*.

If the ridges on both sides of the ending ridge follow its directions or flow trend, the print may be classified as a *plain arch*.

An upthrust then must not only be an ending ridge rising at a sufficient degree from the horizontal plane, but there must also be a space between the ending ridge and the ridge immediately beneath it.

This, however, is not necessary for a short upthrust or spike, or any upthrust, which rises perpendicularly.

In connection with the proper classification to be assigned to those borderline loop-tented arch cases, where an appendage or spike is thrusting out from the recurve, it is necessary to remember, that an appendage or spike abutting upon a recurve at right angles in the space between the shoulders of a loop on the outside, is considered to spoil the recurve.

It must be remembered that the core of a loop may not be placed below the shoulder line. Lacking one of the three characteristics of a loop, these patterns must be classified as *tented arches*.

If the recurve is spoiled by an appendage abutting upon it between the shoulders at a right angle, the pattern must also be classified as a *tented arch*.

One of the requirements of a loop type is that the ridge enters on one side, recurves, and makes its exit on the side from which it entered. This makes it necessary that the ridge passes between the delta and the core. In some patterns the ridge passes between the delta and the core, it does not show any tendency to make its exit on the side from which it entered, and therefore the loop classification is precluded, and it is a *tented arch*.

Tented Arch Pattern Samples

Chapter 5
Whorl Patterns And Whorl Tracing

The Whorl

Whorl type patterns occur in about 30% of all fingerprints. The whorl or numerical value family plays a very important role in the classification of fingerprints. The whorl patterns are:

- The Plain Whorl
- The Central Pocket Loop
- The double Loop
- Accidental

The whorl is that type of pattern in which at least two deltas are present with a recurve in front of each.

The ridges - or some of the ridges - form a more or less circular pattern in this category.

Both a plain whorl and a central pocket loop whorl must have at least one ridge that makes a complete circuit.

Its shape may be spiral, oval or any variation of a circle.

The Plain Whorl

The plain whorl consists of the simplest form of whorl construction and is the most common of the whorl subdivision.

The plain whorl has two deltas and at least one ridge making a complete circuit, which may be spiral, oval, circular, or any variant of a circle. The complete circuit can be a either spiral, circular, oval, or any variation of a complete circle.

An imaginary line drawn between the two deltas *must* touch or cross at least one of the recurving ridges within the inner pattern area.

Every whorl pattern has two lines of flow, which can be described as an imaginary line from the delta to the core.

A whorl pattern must have a free recurve in front of each delta

A recurving ridge, however, which has an appendage connected within the line of flow cannot be constructed as a circuit. An appendage connected at that point is considered to spoil the recurve on that side, and the *pattern is classified as a loop*.

Plain Whorl Pattern Samples

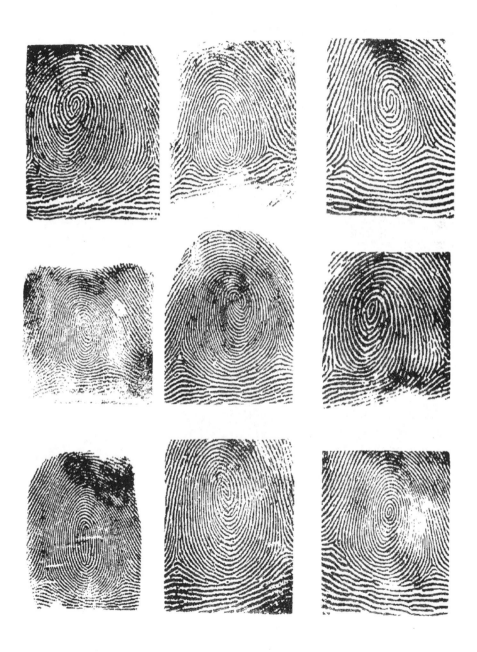

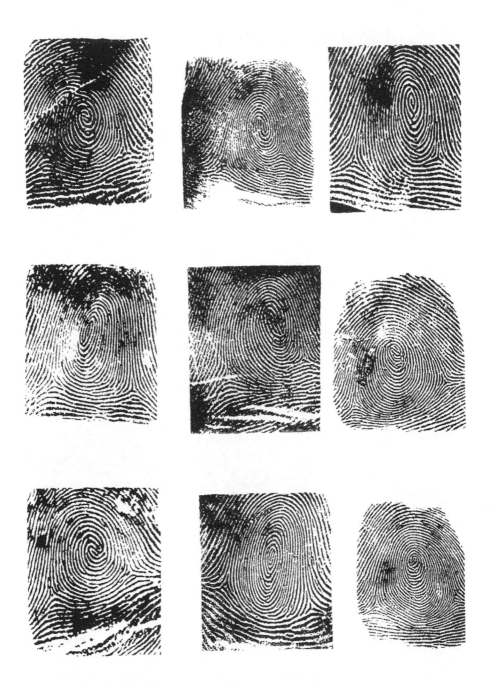

46

Central Pocket Loop Whorl

The central pocket loop type of whorl has two deltas and at least one ridge, which makes or tends to make a complete circuit. The circuit may be spiral, oval, circular, or any variant of a circle. The central pocket loop has the same requirements needed for the plain whorl up to the point of the imaginary line.

An imaginary line drawn between the two deltas must not touch or cross any recurving ridges within the inner pattern area.

A recurving ridge, however, which has an appendage connected within the line of flow and on the delta side cannot be construed as a circuit. An appendage connected at that point is considered to spoil the recurve on that side.

The complete circuits can have the same shape as in the plain whorl, but the only difference is that the central pocket loop pattern circuit imaginary line does not touch a complete circuit.

The central pocket loop does not always have a free recurve in front of both deltas. There is an exception to the complete circuit portion, which is called the *right angle appendage* to the *inner line of flow*. The central pocket loop whorl will usually have one delta higher than the other. The higher delta is nearer the inner pattern area. The imaginary line between the higher delta and the backside of the innermost recurving ridge is considered the *inner line of flow*. In lieu of a recurve in front of the delta in the inner pattern area, an obstruction at right angles to line of flow will suffice. An appendage at right angles to the inner line of flow will take the place of a free recurve in front of the delta.

The inner line of flow is determined by drawing an imaginary line between the inner delta and the center of the innermost recurve or looping ridge.

In the central pocket loop whorl, one or more of the simple recurves of the plain loop type usually recurve a second time to form a pocket within the loop.

The second recurve, however, need not be a continuation of - or even connected with- the first. It may be an independent ridge.

If no second recurve is present, an obstruction at right angles to the inner line of flow is acceptable in lieu of it.

An obstruction may be either curved or straight. A dot, of course, may not be considered an obstruction.

The definition does not require a recurve to cross the line of flow at right angles. The angle needs to be applied to obstructions only.

The recurve or obstruction of the central pocket loop, as that of the plain whorl, must be free of any appendage connected to it at the point crossed by the line of flow and on the delta side.

An appendage at that point is considered to spoil the recurve or obstruction and the pattern would be classified as a loop.

Some central pocket loop patterns even have appendages connected to the recurves, but they are *not connected at the point crossed by the line of flow.*

If one of the *deltas is located on the only recurving* ridge, the pattern would not be classified as a central pocket loop, but as a *loop pattern.*

Even if the pattern possesses one delta and a delta formation, the pattern is classified as a loop because an obstruction does not cross the line of flow at right angles.

If a pattern has two deltas and one or more recurves, but each recurve is spoiled by an appendage connected to it at the point crossed by the line of flow, the pattern is classified as a loop.

If one of the *deltas is located on the only recurving* ridge, the pattern would not be classified as a central pocket loop, but as a *loop pattern.*

Even if the pattern possesses one delta and a delta formation, the pattern is classified as a loop because an obstruction does not cross the line of flow at right angles.

If a pattern has two deltas and one or more recurves, but each recurve is spoiled by an appendage connected to it at the point crossed by the line of flow, the pattern is classified as a loop.

Central Pocket Loop Whorl Pattern Samples

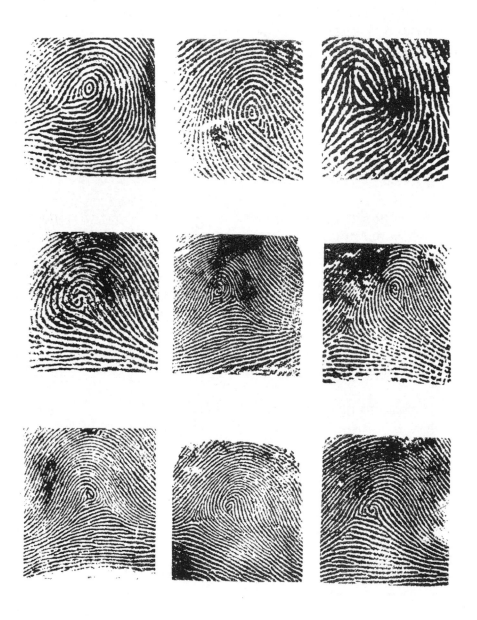

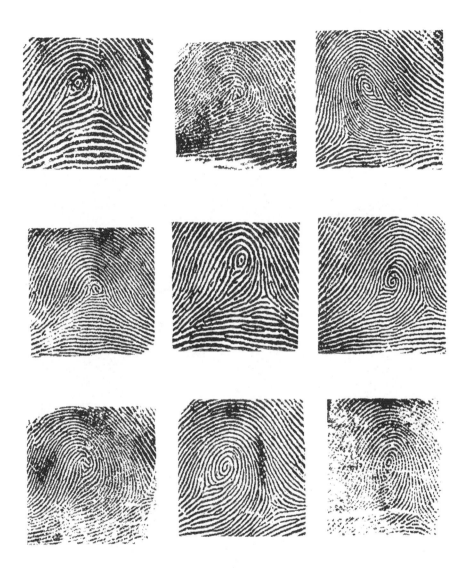

Double Loop Whorl

The definition of a double loop whorl is that it consists of two separate loop formations, with two separate and distinct sets of shoulders, and two deltas. The same right angle appendage between the shoulders that spoils the plain loop pattern will also spoil the double loop whorl pattern. The one requirement not necessary in the double loop whorl pattern is the ridge count across the looping ridge.

The word "separate" does not mean unconnected. An appending ridge may connect the two loops provided that it does not abut at right angles between the shoulders of the loop formation.

The appendage rule for the loop applies also to the double loop whorl. An appendage abutting upon the loop at right angles between the shoulders is considered to spoil the loop, while an appendage, which flows off smoothly, is considered to leave the recurve intact.

The fact that there must be two separate loop formations eliminates from consideration as a double loop the 'S' type core, the interlocking type core, and the formation with one loop inside another.

The loops of a double loop do not have to conform to the requirements of the loop. In other words, no ridge count is necessary.

It is not essential that both sides of a loop are of equal length, and that the two loops be of the same size. Neither is it material from which side the loop enters.

If one side of one loop forms the side of the other, the pattern is classifies as a *plain whorl.*

Double Loop Whorl Pattern Samples

If one side of one loop forms the side of the other, the pattern is classifies as a *plain whorl.*

If the recurves of the loop are spoiled by appendages, the pattern is classified as a *plain loop.*

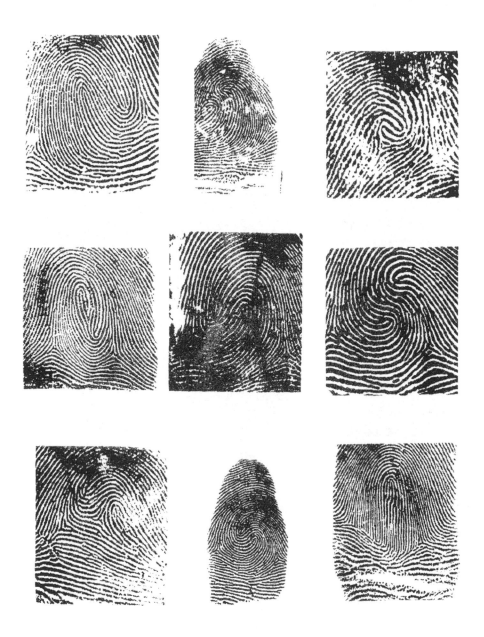

Accidental Whorl

The accidental whorl is a pattern consisting of a combination of two different types of patterns, with the exception of the plain,

- with two or more deltas;

- or pattern which possesses some of the requirements for two or more different types;

- or a pattern, which conforms to none of the definitions.

It may be a combination of *loop and tented arch, loop and whorl, loop and central pocket loop, double loop and central pocket loop,* or *other such combinations.*

The only pattern, which is never part of an accidental combination, is the plain arch, because all fingerprints have an area just below the delta, which has the appearance of a plain arch.

Underneath every pattern there are ridges running from one side to the other, so that if it where not excluded every pattern but the plain arch would be an accidental whorl.

A combination of a loop and tented arch formation must have the loop formation appearing *over* the tented arch.

Any loop and tented arch formation not in this position shall have the loop formation as the preferred pattern.

The overall impression would then be given the classification of either an ulnar or radial loop.

This sub-classification also includes those exceedingly unusual patterns, which may not be placed by definition into any other classes.

Some whorls may be found which contain ridges conforming to more than one of the whorl subdivisions described.

In such cases, the order of preference (if any practical distinction need to be made) should be:

- Accidental Whorl

- Double Loop Whorl

- Central Pocket Loop Whorl

- Plain Whorl

The majority of true accidental whorl patterns are found in the index fingers, whereas the plain arch is mostly found in thumbs.

Accidental Whorl Pattern Samples

Whorl Tracing

While loops are classified according to the number of ridges counted between the delta and core, whorls are traced from delta to delta to determine if the pattern is an inner, outer, or meeting. Whorl tracing always begins from the left delta to the right delta. The technique of whorl tracing depends upon the establishment of the focal points - *the deltas*. Every whorl has two or more.

When the deltas have been located, the ridge emanating from the lower side or point of extreme left delta is traced until the point where the nearest or opposite the extreme delta is, then counted.

If the ridge traced passes inside (above) the right delta, and three or more ridges intervene between the tracing ridge and the delta, the tracing is designated as an **_"inner"_**- **_I._**

If the ridge traced passes outside (below) the right delta, and three or more ridges intervene between the tracing ridge and the right delta, the tracing is designated as an **_"outer"_**- **_O._**

All other tracings are designated as **_"meeting"_**- **_M._**

Tracing begins from the left delta. In no instance is tracing to begin on a type line.

If a short ridge ends immediately the left line is next followed, but this is only because the type line is the next lower ridge. Its status as a type line is independent and has no bearing on the fact that it is being traced.

- It will be noted that the delta is at the point on the first recurve nearest to the center of divergence of the type lines.

- It will further be noted that tracing begins at the point of delta on the left and continues toward the right, passing the inside of the right delta.

When the ridge traced abruptly, and it is determined that the ridge definitely ends, the tracing drops down to the point on the next lower ridge immediately beneath the point where the ridge above ends, continuing from there.

In this connection it should be noted that the rule for dropping to the next lower line applies only when the ridge *definitely* ends.

Short breaks in a ridge which may be due to improper inking, the presence of foreign matter on the ridges, enlarged pores, disease, or worm ridges should not be considered as definite ridge endings.

When the question arises as to whether a break encountered in the ridge tracing as a definite ending, or whether there has been interference wit a natural impression, the whole pattern should be examined to ascertain whether such breaks are general throughout the pattern.

If they are found to be common, consideration should then be given to the possibility that the break is not a definite ridge ending.

Appropriate reference tracing be done in all such cases.

Whenever the ridge traced bifurcates, the rule for tracing requires that the lower limb or branch proceeding from the bifurcation be followed.

Accidentals often possess three or more deltas. In tracing them, only the extreme deltas are considered, the tracing beginning at the extreme left delta and proceeding toward the extreme right delta.

In a **double loop whorl** or **accidental whorl** the problem of where to stop tracing is sometimes present.

The rule is, when tracing passes inside of the right delta, stop at the nearest point to the right delta on the upward trend.

If no upward trend is present, continue tracing until a point opposite the right delta, or the delta itself, is reached.

Chapter 6

The Classification Formula and Extension

At this point it is necessary to mention that when prints are classified, markings are indicated at the bottom of each finger block on the fingerprint card to reflect the type.

Classification Symbols

The following symbols are used:

- Under the index fingers the appropriate capital letters should be placed for every pattern except the ulnar loop.

- Under all fingers, the appropriate small letter should be placed for every pattern except the ulnar loop and the whorl as follows:

  Arch .... a

  Tented Arch .... t

  Radial Loop .... r

- Ulnar loops in any finger are designated by a diagonal line (/ or \ ) slanting in the direction of the loop.

- Whorls in any finger are designated by the letter "*W*".

- Amputated or bandaged fingers are classified the same as the opposite fingers. If both of the same kind fingers are amputated, they become "*Meet Whorl*".

Pattern Codes

Pattern Codes		
Index Fingers	Arch	A
	Tented arch	T
	Radial loop	R
	Ulnar loop	U
	Whorl	W
All others	Whorl	w
	Arch	a
Letter Code…	Tented arch	t
Used in blocking out a Fingerprint Card	Radial loop	r
	Ulnar loop	\ (Right Hand)
		/ (Left Hand)

Classification Divisions

The classification formula may be composed of the following divisions:

1. Key
2. Major
3. Primary
4. Secondary
5. Sub-Secondary
6. Final

Key	Major	Primary	Secondary	Sub-Secondary	Final
Count of first Loop (Except) Little Finger)	Both Thumbs I.M.O. SML (Letters)	Numerical Value of Whorls 16,16,8,8,4 4,2,2,1,1 + 1	Pattern in Index Finger (Capital) Letters)	Index Middle Ring I.M.O I , O (Letters only)	Count of Little Finger (Loop)

Sample Classification					
Key	Major Division	Primary	Secondary Classification	Sub-Secondary	Final
20	M	I	U	IOI	10
	L	I	U	IOI	

Key	Major	Primary	Secondary	Second Sub-Secondary Classification	Final
4	O	5	U	IOI	10
	I	17	U	IOI	

The Key

The Key is obtained by counting the ridges of the first loop appearing on the fingerprint card, beginning with the right thumb, except the little finger, which is never considered for the key.

If there is no loop on the card, the first whorl is counted. The ridge count is obtained from the left delta to the core.

The Key, no matter where found, is always placed to the extreme left of the numerator of the classification formula.

Major Division for Loops

The major division is obtained from both thumbs right over left, and is placed just to the right of the Key in the classification formula. Where whorls appear in the thumbs, the major division reflects the whorl tracings.

For example, a major division "I" over "M" in the primary "5" over "17" would reflect an inner-traced whorl over a meet-traced whorl in the thumbs.

Where loops appear in the thumbs, however, a table is used to translate the ridge counts into the small, medium, or large groups, designated by the letters "S", "M", "L".

An expanding table is used for the right thumb when large-count loops appear in the left thumb.

The left thumb denominator is placed below the right thumb denominator in the classification formula.

This table is used because it affords a more equitable distribution of prints as a whole, for filing purposes within the groups indicated.

Right Hand				
Thumb	**Index**	**Middle**	**Ring**	**Little**
When left Thumb is 16 or less... 0 – 11 = S 12 – 16 = M 17 +　　= S				
When left Thumb is 17 or more... 0 – 17 = S 18 – 22 = M 23 +　　= S				
Left Hand				
When left Thumb is 16 or less... 0 – 11 = S 12 – 16 = M 17 +　　= S				

The Table for Major Division of Loops:

Left thumb denominator

0 to 11, inclusive, S (small)

Right thumb denominator

0 to11, inclusive, S (small)

12 to 16, inclusive, M (medium)

17 or more ridges, L (large)

Left thumb denominator

12 to 16, inclusive, M (medium)

Right thumb denominator

0 to 11, inclusive, S (small)

12 to 16, inclusive, M (medium)

17 or more ridges, L (large)

Left thumb denominator

17 or more ridges, L (large)

Right thumb denominator

0 to 17, inclusive, S (small)

18 to 22, inclusive, M (medium)

23 or more ridges, L (large)

The Primary

For the purpose of obtaining the primary classification, numerical values are assigned to each of the ten fingers.

Wherever a whorl appears it assumes the value of the space in which it was found. Spaces in which types of patterns are present are disregarded in computing the primary.

The values are assigned as follows:

Fingers No. 1 and No. 2	16
Fingers No. 3 and No. 4	8
Fingers No. 5 and No. 6	4
Fingers No. 7 and No. 8	2
Fingers No. 9 and No. 1	1

	Thumb	Index	Middle	Ring	Little	
Right Hand	16	16	8	8	4	
	1	2	3	4	5	**+1**
Left Hand	4	2	2	1	1	
	6	7	8	9	10	

These Numerical Values…

Are assigned to each square on the fingerprint card. "1" is added to each of the total number of squares in which whorls appear, counting the even-numbered (on top) and the odd numbers (on the bottom) squares separately.

The Secondary

The secondary division is obtained from both index fingers and is placed just to the right of the primary in the classification formula.

After the primary the entire remaining portion of the classification formula is based upon the arrangement of the impressions appearing in the right hand as the numerator over the impression appearing in the left hand as the denominator.

The secondary classification appears just to the right of the fractional numerals, which represents the primary. It is shown in the formula by capital letters representing the basic type of patterns appearing in the index fingers of each hand, that of the right hand the numerator and that of the left hand being the denominator.

There are five basic types of patterns that can appear:

1.	Arch	**A**
2.	Tented Arch	**T**
3.	Radial Loop	**R**
4.	Ulnar Loop	U
5.	Whorl	**W**

Secondary classification (small letter group):

Prints with an arch or tented arch in any finger or a radial loop in any except the index fingers constitute the small letter group.

The Sub-Secondary

The sub-secondary division is obtained from the index fingers, middle fingers and the ring fingers and is placed just to the right of the secondary in the classification formula.

In classifying prints it is necessary to subdivide the secondary groups (Grouping of loops and whorls).

This is accomplished by grouping according to the ridge counts of loops and the ridge tracing of whorls. The first of the groups filed in order, which will be necessary to so subdivide, would ordinarily be the group where no small letters appear.

Ridge counts are translated into small and large, represented by symbols "I" and "O". Each ridge count must consist of two characters.

Secondary classification (small letter group):

Prints with an arch or tented arch in any finger or a radial loop in any except the index fingers constitute the small letter group.

Index finger: A ridge count of 01 to 09 must be preceded by an "O"; and a ridge count of 10 and over must be preceded by an "I".

Middle finger: A ridge count of 01 to 10 must be preceded by an "O"; and a ridge count of 11 and over must be preceded by an "I".

Ring finger: A ridge count of 01 to 13 must be preceded by an "O"; and a ridge count of 14 and over must be preceded by an "I".

The whorl tracings are brought up as "I", "M", or "O" denoting "inner", "meeting", or "outer" ridge tracings of the whorl types.

Only six fingers may be involved in the sub-secondary - numbers **2**, **3**, **4**, **7**, **8**, and **9**.

	Thumb	Index	Middle	Ring	Little
Right Hand		01 - 09 = I 10 & Over = O	01 - 10 = I 11 & Over = O	01 - 13 = I 14 & Over = O	
Left Hand		01 - 09 = I 10 & Over = O	01 - 10 = I 11 & Over = O	01 - 13 = I 14 & Over = O	

Sub-Secondary Classification

The Final

The final division is obtained from the ridge count of the loop of the right little finger, and is placed just to the right of the sub-secondary in the classification formula.

If a loop does not appear in the right little finger, a loop in the left little finger may be used.

If no loops appear in the little fingers, a whorl may be used to obtain a final, counting from the left delta to core in the right hand and from the right delta to core in the left hand.

If there are two or more cores, usually applies to accidental whorls, the ridge count is made from the left delta (right hand) or the right delta (left hand) to the core which is the least number of ridges distant from that delta.

An exception is made in the case of a double loop. The double loop is counted from the delta to the core of the upright loop. Where loops of a double loop are horizontal, the nearest core is used.

Should both little fingers be an "a" or "t", no final is used.

The use of a whorl in a little finger for a final is required only in connection with a large group or collection if prints, such as the 32 over 32 primary.

The Second Sub-Secondary (Extensions)

When a group of fingerprints becomes so large that it is cumbersome and unwieldy, even though fully extended, it can be subdivided further by using a second sub-secondary division. The second sub-secondary is brought up into the classification formula directly above the sub-secondary, and for which the symbols "S", "M", and "L" are used.

The following table is used:

Index: 01 to 05, inclusive, S

06 to 12, inclusive, M

13 or more,   L

Middle: 01 to 08, inclusive, S

09 to 14, inclusive, M

15 or more,   L

Ring: 01 to 10, inclusive, S

11 to 18, inclusive, M

19 or more,   L

	Thumb	Index	Middle	Ring	Little
Right Hand		01 – 05 = S 06 – 11 = M 12 + = L	01 – 08 = S 09 – 14 = M 15 + = L	01 – 10 = S 11 – 18 = M 19 + = L	
Left Hand		01 – 05 = S 06 – 11 = M 12 + = L	01 – 08 = S 09 – 14 = M 15 + = L	01 – 10 = S 11 – 18 = M 19 + = L	
		Second Sub-Secondary Classification			

Classification Examples

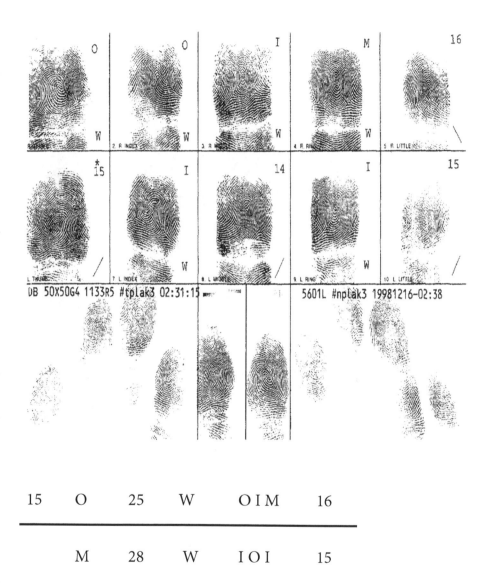

15	O	25	W	O I M	16
	M	28	W	I O I	15

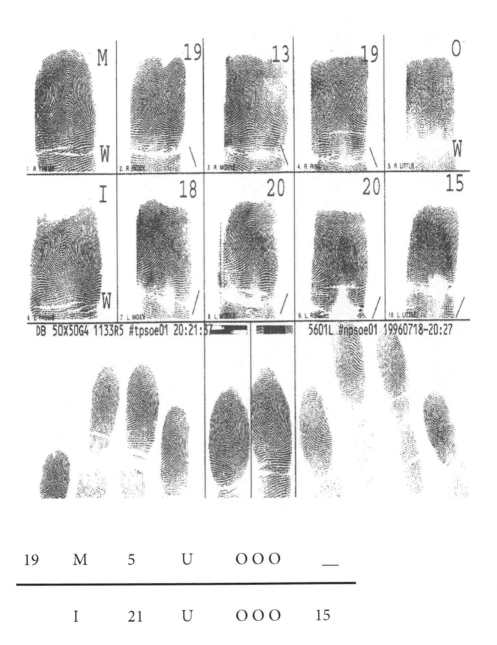

19   M   5   U   O O O   __

I   21   U   O O O   15

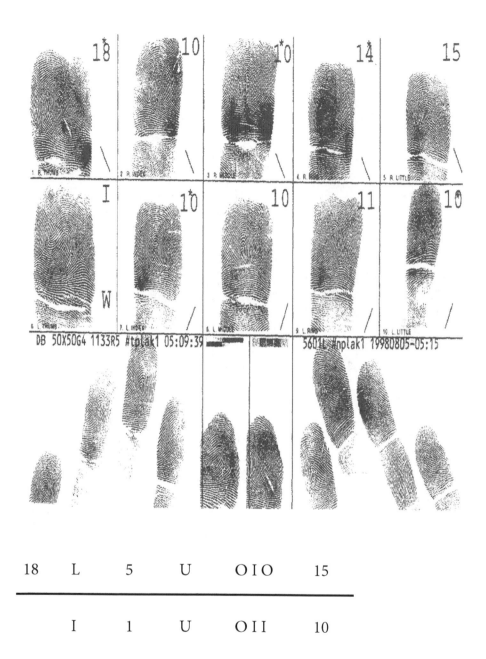

18	L	5	U	O I O	15
I	1	U	O I I	10	

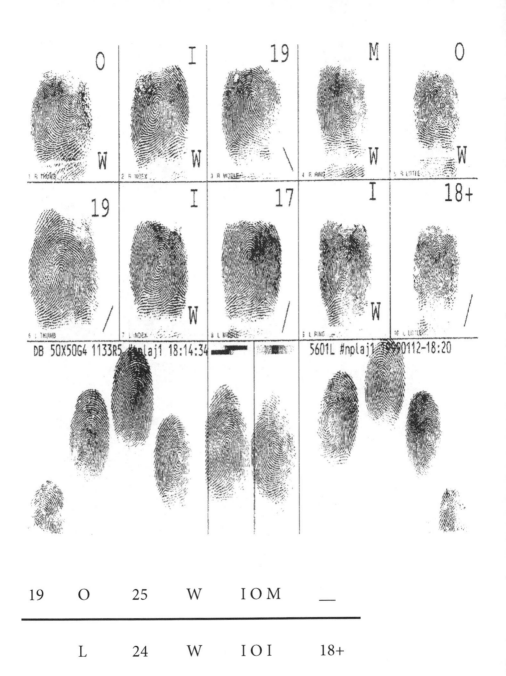

19	O	25	W	I O M	__
	L	24	W	I O I	18+

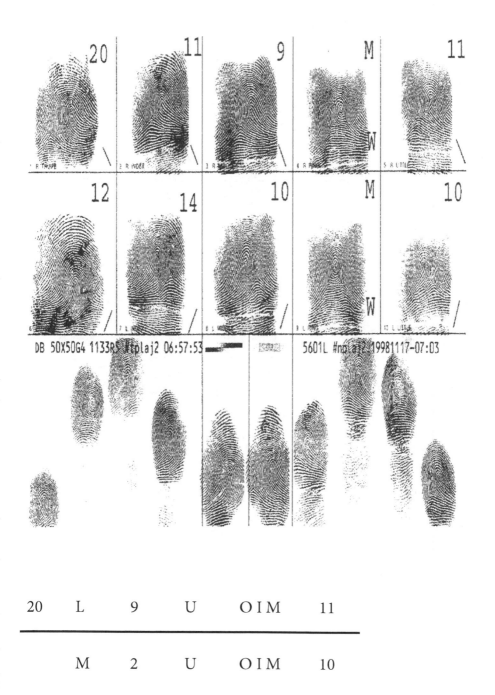

20	L	9	U	O I M	11
	M	2	U	O I M	10

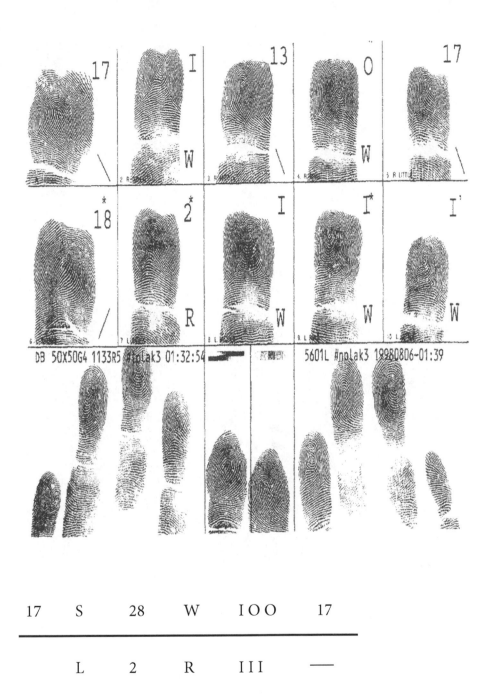

17   S   28   W   I O O   17

    L   2   R   III   ——

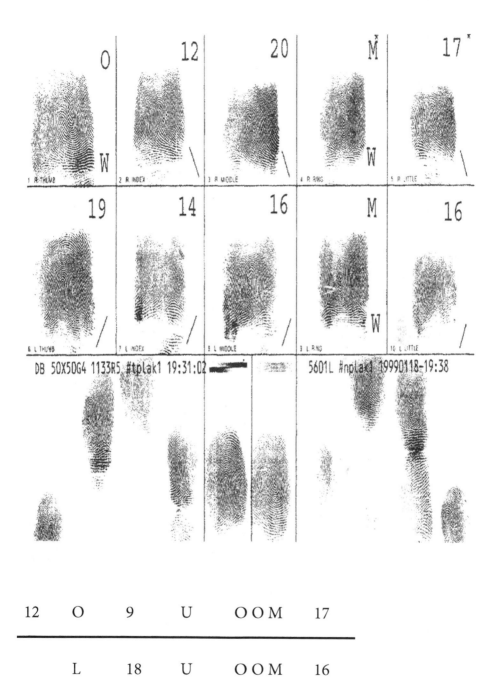

12	O	9	U	O O M	17
	L	18	U	O O M	16

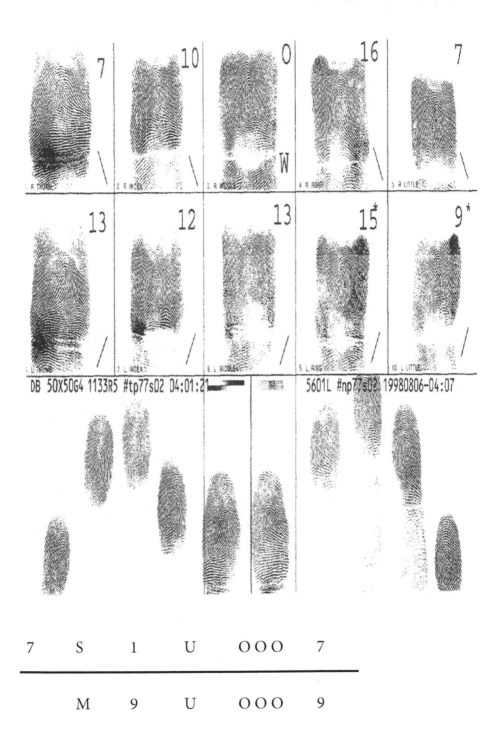

7	S	1	U	O O O	7
	M	9	U	O O O	9

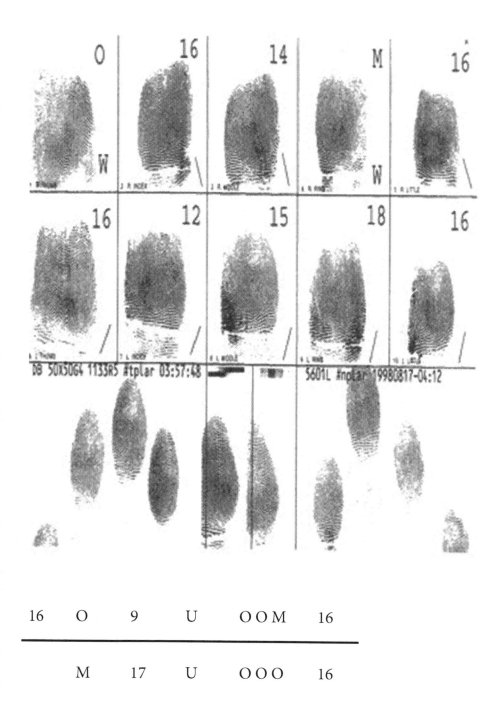

16   O   9   U   O O M   16

M   17   U   O O O   16

Chapter 7 – Referencing And Small Letter Classification

Factors that make it necessary to reference are:

- Variation in individual judgment and eyesight.
- The amount of ink used.
- The amount of pressure used in taking the prints.
- The difference in width of the rolled impression.
- Skin diseases
- Worn ridges due to age or occupation.
- Temporary or permanent scars
- Bandaged fingers
- Crippled hands
- Amputations

For the highest degree of accuracy, all rolled impressions should be checked by the plain impressions, which generally are not distorted by pressure.

This also helps prevent error caused by the reversal or mixing of rolled impressions out of their proper order.

If there is any doubt as to which of two or more classifications should be assigned to a given pattern, it is given the preferred classification and reference searches are conducted in all other possible classifications.

If both of the same kind fingers are amputated, they become "Meet Whorl".

For example: (a) 1 A   (b) 1 A   and   1   A
                 ‾‾‾‾‾‾   ‾‾‾‾‾   ‾‾‾‾‾‾‾
                 1 Aa   1 At   1 Ar

If on a print with the preferred classification it is questionable whether the left middle finger should be a plain arch, or a radial loop, the print is searched in the group (a), and reference searches are conducted in the (b) groups.

For further illustration, a print is given a primary classification of 1 over 1, although the ridge detail on the right thumb is so formed as to resemble a whorl. The search is completed first in the preferred primary classification (c) and a reference search is then conducted in the primary (d).

(c)   1   (d)   1
      ‾‾‾   ‾‾‾
       1   17

All ridge counts that are "line counts", i.e., when one or more or one less count would change the designation of the loop from I to O or from S to M, etc., must be searched in both groups.

(e)   16   M   1   U   I I I   10
      ‾‾‾‾‾‾‾‾‾‾‾‾‾‾‾‾‾‾‾‾‾‾‾‾‾‾‾‾‾‾‾
       M   1   U   I I I   14

84

(f) | M 1 U I O I | L 1 U III | L 1 U I O I |
     | M 1 U I I I | M 1 U III | M 1U III |

For example in a print classified (e), if the ridge count of the right middle finger is 10 and the count in the right thumb would be searched first as classified, then reference searches would be conducted in the (f) groups.

When there is doubt concerning the tracing of a whorl, it should be treated in the same fashion. For example, if in the classification (g) doubt exists as to whether the tracing in the right thumb might not be a "meet", the print would be searched as classified and a reference search would be conducted in (h).

(g) | O 5 U | (h) | M 5 U |
     | I 17 U | | I 17 U |

If there is no doubt concerning the ridge count used for the final, it is enough to search out for the group only those prints containing a final within 2 ridge counts on each side of the final on the print being searched.

Referencing Examples

6	S	1	U	III	8	Ref:	6	S 1 U	OIO	8
	S	1	U	III				S 1 U	III	4

6	9 10	5	13 14	8
\	\	\	\	\
4	3	9	12	4
/	/	/	/	/

15	S	9	U	I I O	10	Ref:	15 M 9 U OOO	10
	L	3	W	I I O	19		M 3 W III	19

15	9 10	10 11	O	10
\	\	\	w	\
17 16	I	4	14 13	19
/	W	/	/	/

Small Letter Classification

Prints with an **arch** or **tented arch** in any finger or a **radial loop** in any except the index fingers constitute the small-letter group of the secondary classification.

        a   arch

        t   tented arch

        r   radial

1. If either or both thumb patterns are an **arch** or **tented arch**, then there is **no major** in the classification formula.

2. If there is no major, the key is put into parenthesis ( ).

3. The small letter will appear between the primary and the secondary.

4. Never show another pattern other than **r**, **t**, and/or an a, between the secondary and small letter, use a dash [–] instead.

5. Do not force a major, if there are arches or tented arches in the thumb patterns then there is no major.

6. If there are two or more the same small letters, instead of putting for example "**a a a**" put **3a**, or "**t t t**" put **3t**, and for "**r r r**" put **3r**.

Such "small letters", with the exception of those appearing in the index finger, are brought up into the classification formula in their proper relative position immediately adjacent to the index fingers.

A dash is used to indicate the absence of each small letter between the index fingers and another small letter or between two small letters (a).

(a) $\dfrac{1 \ \ aUa\text{-}t}{1 \ \ \ R\text{-}a}$ and $\dfrac{1 \ aU\text{-}t}{1 \ U\text{-}a}$

If an arch or tented arch or a radial loop would appear in the middle, ring or little finger of the hand, the small letter representing such a pattern would be placed on the classification line to the right of the secondary in the numerator column if the letter is present in the right hand, and in the denominator column if in the left hand.

When two or more small letters of the same type occur immediately adjacent to each other, they are indicated as (b).

(b) $\dfrac{1 \ \ rU\text{-}2a}{1 \ \ tU3a}$ and $\dfrac{1 \ \ aTa\text{-}a}{1 \ \ tA2at}$

The small letter groups are of vital importance to the classification system, as they are of relatively infrequent occurrence, constituting approximately 7 to 10 percent of all patterns.

Since these patterns are of such rare occurrence, their very presence often enables the classifier to dispense with the usual sub-secondary classification and the major division, which in the majority of cases are used in the larger groups.

Small Letter Classification Examples

$$\frac{6 \quad S \quad 1 \quad U \quad - - t}{S \quad 1 \quad R \quad 2t - 9}$$

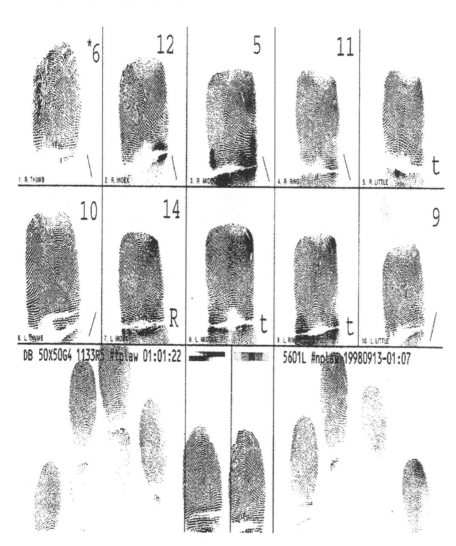

19 L 1 U a 5
M 1 U a 2t -

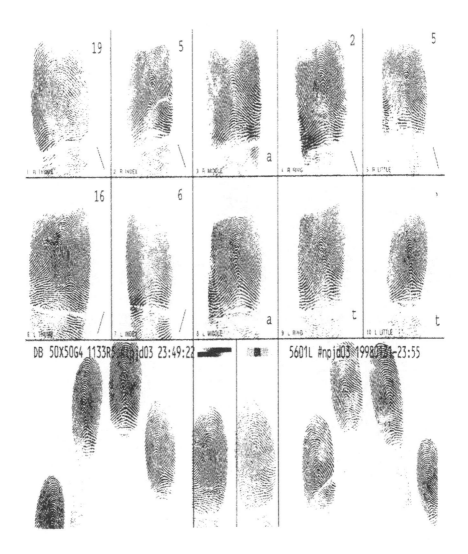

24	L	1	T	a	6
	L	1	A	2a	10

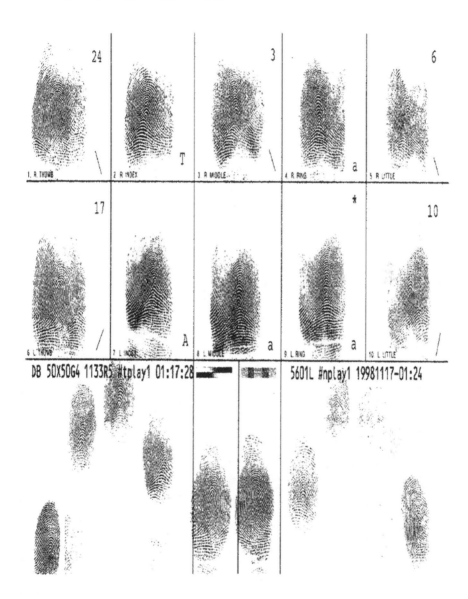

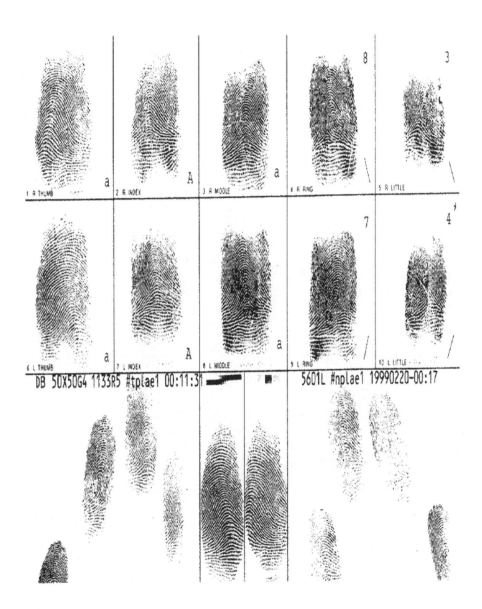

(5)   1 a R - - a   -
 1 A t   7

5	12	6	
a	R	\	\	a
8	12		11	7
/	A	t	/	/

(15)   1 U a t a   -
   1aU t r   8

15	15			
\	\	a	t	a
	4		16	8
a	/	t	t	/

93

(15) O   5 U 2a   -
         15 U 2t   -

O	15		14	
w	\	a	\	a
I	8		13	
w	/	t	/	t

15 O 6 U 2a   -
   I 17 U t 12

O	15		14	
w	\	a	\	a
I	12		8	I
				12
w	/	t	/	w

(14) 1 t A t 2 a
     1 r A t a t

t	A	t	a	a
14				
r	A	t	a	t

(6)   1 a T t - -   8
      1 a R - - r   2

			6	8
a	T	t	\	\
4	5		8	2
a	R	/	/	r

6   O 5 T t   10
 I   21 R - - r   2

			6	I
				10
O				
w	T	t	\	w
I	3	5	8	2
w	R	/	/	r

(5) 5 a T   II   16
 5 R   III   2

		5	6	I
				16
a	T	\	\	w
I	3	5	8	2
w	R	/	/	/

Chapter 8 - Coding

NCIC Coding

The **National Crime Information Center** (NCIC) is a computerized information system established as a service to all law enforcement agencies – local, state and Federal.

To alleviate problems existing due to the various methods of fingerprint classification, the following method was devised and should be utilized in classifying fingerprints for entry into the into the FPC (NCIC Fingerprint Classification) field of wanted persons record format.

This is a 20-character field seen below:

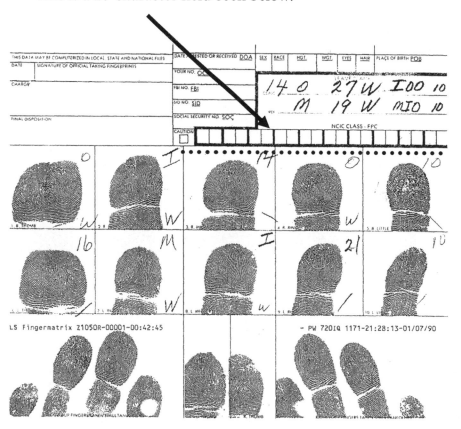

As is well known, the fingers are numbered beginning with the right thumb as number 1, and continuing through number 10 with the left little finger.

Two characters are to be used for each finger as shown below:

Plain Arch ------------- **AA**

Tented Arch ----------- **TT**

Radial Loop ----------- Two numeric characters. Determine **actual ridge count** and **add 50.**

Ulnar Loop ------------ Two numeric characters indicating **actual ridge count**. If the ridge count is under 10 use 09, 08, etc.

Plain Whorl ----------- Enter **"P"** followed by the **tracing** of the whorl.

- Inner tracing ----------------- **P I**
- Outer tracing ----------------- **PO**
- Meeting tracing ------------- **PM**

Central Pocket Loop -   Enter "C" followed by the **tracing** of
the whorl.

- Inner tracing ---------------- **C I**
- Outer tracing --------------- **CO**
- Meeting tracing ------------- **CM**

Double Loop Whorl - Enter "**d**" followed by the tracing of the
                              whorl (use small letter for the "d")

- Inner tracing ----------------- **d I**
- Outer tracing ---------------- **d O**
- Meeting tracing ------------- **d M**

In double loop whorl pattern the small letter "**d**" is utilized to
prevent identifying the capital "**D**" with the letter "**O**". If typed or
machine printed, the small letter "d" would be put as a capital
letter "D".

Accidental Whorl ---- Enter "**X**" followed by the **tracing** of the
                              whorl.

- Inner tracing ----------------- **X I**
- Outer tracing ---------------- **XO**
- Meeting tracing -------------- **XM**

Missing / Amputated finger -------- **XX**

   Used only in instances of missing and totally/partly amputated
fingers making it impossible to accurately classify an impression.

It is recognized that under the Henry System of classifying fingerprints, if a finger is missing or amputated, it is given the classification identical with the opposite finger. However this should not be done in the NCIC FPC, since precise identity of the finger(s) missing or amputated is not preserved.

Completely Scarred or Mutilated Patterns ------------------ **SR**

Use "**d**" only when the fingerprint cannot be accurately classified due to complete scarring or mutilation. The procedure of assigning the opposite finger should not be used.

WCDX Extensions

Plain Whorl ----------------------------------**W**
Central Pocket Loop Whorl ---------------- **C**
Double Loop Whorl ------------------------ **D**
Whorl Accidental --------------------------- **X**

Baseline and Core

Also referred as Core and AXIS.

The crease is the bend of the finger and that is where we find the baseline, also known as the guideline.

The baseline is where the print is showing a white space, as seen in the examples below.

The examples also show how the area is defined for the computer (AXIS) to search.

This is the way the computer knows which direction the print pattern is flowing.

NCF Coding

Numerical Coded Fingerprint (NCF) is used by the Los Angeles Police Department.

The coding is shown below:

Ulnar Loop ----------- 400 + the ridge count of the loop

Radial Loop ---------- 300 + the ridge count of the loop

Arch ----------------- 100

Angle Tented Arch -- 210

Upthrust Arch ------- 220

Loop Type Arch ----- 230

Whorl ---------------- 500

       Inner ---------- 500 + the ridge count

       Meeting ------- 500 + 30 + the ridge count

       Outer --------- 500 + 60 + the ridge count

Central Pocket Loop Whorl --- 600

      Inner   ----------------- 600 + the ridge count

      Meeting   --------------- 600 + 30 + the ridge count

      Outer   ---------------- 600 + 60 + the ridge count

Double Loop Whorl ------------ 700

      Inner   ------------------- 700 + the ridge count

      Meeting   ---------------- 700 + 30 + the ridge count

      Outer   ------------------ 700 + 60 + the ridge count

Accidental   -------------------- 800

	PI	PM	DL	CPL
12	10	6	14	11
412	510	536	714	611
\	W	w	w	w
100	210	800	415	230
a	A	x	/	a
Arch	ATA	Accidental	15	LTA

103

Chapter 9
Palm Prints And Foot Prints

Palm Prints

This chapter addresses the importance in understanding the area of latent palm prints. Fingerprint search technology advances have added palm prints cards to their databases. Arrestees do not just have their fingerprints scanned into the databases; they also scan the palms of both hands.

Knowledge of both fingerprint and palm print patterns physical features can be of tremendous benefit in crime scene investigation. The ability to recognize the major friction ridge area of a palm print pattern in addition to fingerprint patterns can be critical for print identification.

Majority of palms have common attributes that are not gender or hand specific. Both male and female, right or left hand, have the same types of ridge and crease formations located in the same areas of the palm.

Three major areas of the palm

The palmer surface of the hand is divided into three major areas, which are the Thenar, the Hypothenar, and the Interdigital.

The **thenar** is the area associated with the *thumb or radial* side of the palm. The **hypothenar** is associated with the *little finger or ulnar* side of the palm. The **interdigital** area is found in *the area directly beneath the fingers.*

The ridge flow of the palm separates the three major areas of the palm. The ridge flow also correlates very closely with the major crease formations of the palm as well.

Primary Ridge Flow

In the **thenar area** the primary flow of ridges form a semi-circular formation around the thumb. The ridges enter into the hand from above the thumb, flow down into the thenar, then curve and exit to the bottom of the hand. This general "half-moon" flow of ridges is very consistent for the thenar area and is one of the largest ridge flow clues found on the palmar surface of the hand.

In the **hypothenar area** of the palm the primary ridge flow of ridges flow downward in a diagonal direction from the center of the hand to the edge of the hand. The ridges flow down and out of the hand and exit the side of the hand as opposed to the bottom of the hand like they do in the thenar area.

In the **interdigital area** of the palm the primary ridge flow begins between the base of the index finger and the middle finger, and flows across the upper section of the hand. It does so in a sweeping motion culminating with a mounded area of ridges directly beneath the base of the little finger before it exits the hand on the ulnar side of the palm. This long falling flow of ridges is consistent in the majority of interdigital areas is called the "waterfall" due to its cascading appearance in this area of the palm.

It is common to find a total of four deltas in the interdigital area, one associated in some way with the finger closest to it. These deltas have physical features that are associated with the finger that it is possible to examine portions of them and determine not only which hand they came from, but also under which finger

Primary Ridge Flow Illustration

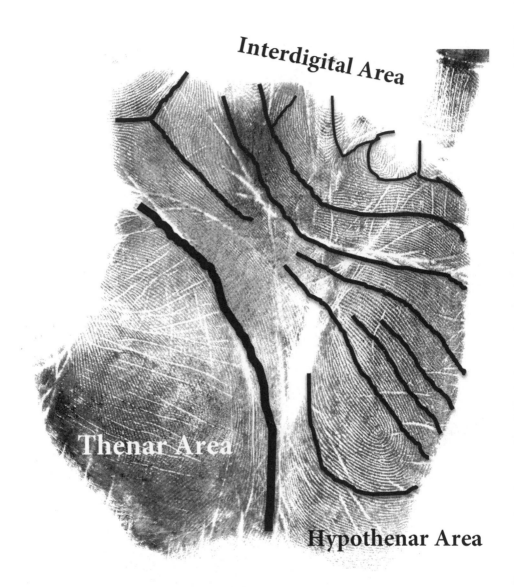

Interdigital Area

Thenar Area

Hypothenar Area

Palm Print Definitions Illustration

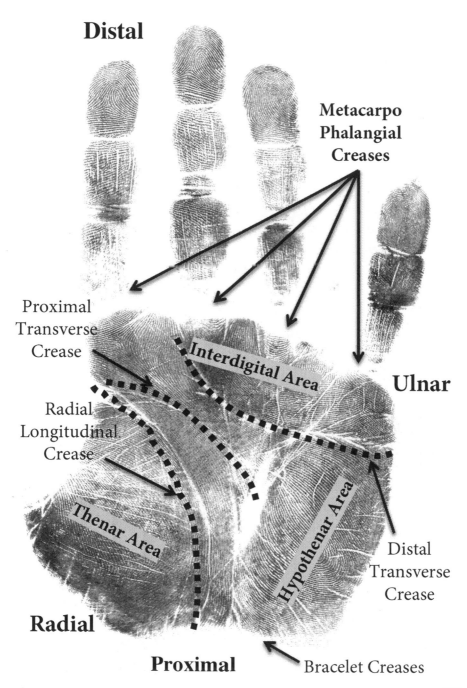

Distal

Metacarpo
Phalangial
Creases

Proximal
Transverse
Crease

Interdigital Area

Ulnar

Radial
Longitudinal
Crease

Thenar Area

Hypothenar Area

Distal
Transverse
Crease

Radial

Proximal

Bracelet Creases

Foot Print

Friction ridge skin present on the soles of the feet and toes (plantar surfaces) is as unique in its ridge detail as are the fingers and palms (palmar surfaces). Sole and toe impressions can be used for identification in the same manner as finger and palm prints. Footprint (toe and sole friction ridge skin) evidence has been admitted in courts in the United States since 1934.

An actual footprint can be checked and matched to an existing print on record, such as one from a birth certificate. The footprints of infants, along with the thumb or index finger prints of mothers, are still commonly recorded in hospitals to assist in verifying the identity of infants. Often, the only identifiable ridge detail that can be seen on a baby's foot is from the large toe or adjacent to the large toe.

It is not uncommon for military records of flight personnel to include bare foot inked impressions. Friction ridge skin protected inside flight boots tends to survive the trauma of a plane crash (and accompanying fire) better than fingers.

Foot Print Definitions Illustration

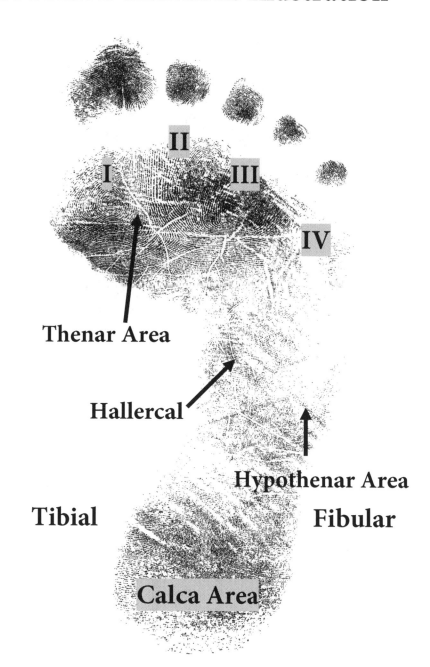

II

I

III

IV

Thenar Area

Hallercal

Hypothenar Area

Tibial

Fibular

Calca Area

Chapter 10 - Sequencing

Sequencing for Filing

The sequence must be arranged properly at all times to make the most accurate work possible. Prints are sequenced and filed in this order according to:

I. **Primary:**

$$\frac{1}{1} \quad \text{to} \quad \frac{32}{32}$$

In the primary classification the denominator remains constant until all numerator figures have been exhausted from **1 to 32**. All prints with the **primary 1 over 1** are filed together.

These are followed by *2 over 1, 3 over 1, 4 over 1, etc., until 32 over 2* is reached.

Eventually, through the use of each numerator figure and the elimination of each numerator over each denominator, the **32 over 32 primary** will be reached.

Even in the smaller collection of fingerprints, it will be found that the groups which are arranged under individual primaries filed in sequence, from 1 over 1 to 32 over 32, will be too voluminous for expeditious searching.

II. Secondary:

a. Secondary small-letter group:

$$\frac{A}{A} \quad \text{to} \quad \frac{rW3r}{rW3r}$$

Most intricate of all the individual sequences is the small letter sequence. It is less difficult if the following method is used:

1. Sequence according to the patterns in the index fingers, grouped.

$$\frac{A}{A} \quad \text{to} \quad \frac{W}{W}$$

25 possible combinations can appear in the index finger when small letters are present. They are as follows:

$\frac{A}{A}$	$\frac{T}{A}$	$\frac{R}{A}$	$\frac{U}{A}$	$\frac{W}{A}$
$\frac{A}{T}$	$\frac{T}{T}$	$\frac{R}{T}$	$\frac{U}{T}$	$\frac{W}{T}$
$\frac{A}{R}$	$\frac{T}{R}$	$\frac{R}{R}$	$\frac{U}{R}$	$\frac{W}{R}$
$\frac{A}{U}$	$\frac{T}{U}$	$\frac{R}{U}$	$\frac{U}{U}$	$\frac{W}{U}$
$\frac{A}{W}$	$\frac{T}{W}$	$\frac{R}{W}$	$\frac{U}{W}$	$\frac{W}{W}$

Within each group sequence:

a. The denominator, by
    1) Count of small letters (lesser preceding the greater)
    2) Position of the small letters (those to the left preceding those to the right)
    3) Type of small letter (sequence a, t, r)

b. The numerator by -
    1) Count
    2) Position
    3) Type

$$\frac{A}{A} \quad \text{precedes} \quad \frac{T}{A}$$

$$\frac{A}{rAt} \quad \text{precedes} \quad \frac{A}{A3t}$$

$$\frac{A}{aA} \quad \text{precedes} \quad \frac{A}{Aa}$$

$$\frac{A}{At} \quad \text{precedes} \quad \frac{A}{Ar}$$

$$\frac{aA}{aAr} \quad \text{precedes} \quad \frac{aAa}{aAr}$$

$$\frac{rA}{aA2a} \quad \text{precedes} \quad \frac{Ar}{aA2a}$$

$$\frac{aAtat}{tA3r} \quad \text{precedes} \quad \frac{aAtar}{tA3r}$$

At this point it should be noted that it might be easier to use only a portion of the classification formula in the filing sequence regarding small files. Only those parts of the filing sequence necessary should be used along with the final key.

III. Sub-Secondary

$$\frac{\text{III}}{\text{III}} \quad \text{to} \quad \frac{\text{OOO}}{\text{OOO}}$$

The sequence of the sub-secondary is as follows:

$\dfrac{\text{III}}{\text{III}}$	$\dfrac{\text{IIM}}{\text{III}}$	$\dfrac{\text{IIO}}{\text{III}}$	$\dfrac{\text{IMI}}{\text{III}}$	$\dfrac{\text{IMM}}{\text{III}}$
$\dfrac{\text{IMO}}{\text{III}}$	$\dfrac{\text{IOI}}{\text{III}}$	$\dfrac{\text{IOM}}{\text{III}}$	$\dfrac{\text{IOO}}{\text{III}}$	$\dfrac{\text{MII}}{\text{III}}$
$\dfrac{\text{MIM}}{\text{III}}$	$\dfrac{\text{MIO}}{\text{III}}$	$\dfrac{\text{MMI}}{\text{III}}$	$\dfrac{\text{MMM}}{\text{III}}$	$\dfrac{\text{MMO}}{\text{III}}$
$\dfrac{\text{MOI}}{\text{III}}$	$\dfrac{\text{MOM}}{\text{III}}$	$\dfrac{\text{MOO}}{\text{III}}$	$\dfrac{\text{OII}}{\text{III}}$	$\dfrac{\text{OIM}}{\text{III}}$
$\dfrac{\text{OIO}}{\text{III}}$	$\dfrac{\text{OMI}}{\text{III}}$	$\dfrac{\text{OMM}}{\text{III}}$	$\dfrac{\text{OMO}}{\text{III}}$	$\dfrac{\text{OOI}}{\text{III}}$
$\dfrac{\text{OOM}}{\text{III}}$	$\dfrac{\text{OOO}}{\text{III}}$	*etc., to*		$\dfrac{\text{OOO}}{\text{OOO}}$

Each numerator in turn becomes the denominator for the complete sequence of numerators as listed above.

IV. Major

The following sequence is used when loops appear in both thumbs:

$$\frac{S}{S} \quad \frac{M}{S} \quad \frac{L}{S} \quad \frac{S}{M} \quad \frac{M}{M} \quad \frac{L}{M} \quad \frac{S}{L} \quad \frac{M}{L} \quad \frac{L}{L}$$

When whorls appear in both thumbs the sequence is:

$$\frac{I}{I} \quad \frac{M}{I} \quad \frac{O}{I} \quad \frac{I}{M} \quad \frac{M}{M} \quad \frac{O}{M} \quad \frac{I}{O} \quad \frac{M}{O} \quad \frac{O}{O}$$

When a whorl appears in the right thumb and a loop in the left, the sequence is:

$$\frac{I}{S} \quad \frac{M}{S} \quad \frac{O}{S} \quad \frac{I}{M} \quad \frac{M}{M} \quad \frac{O}{M} \quad \frac{I}{L} \quad \frac{M}{L} \quad \frac{O}{L}$$

When a loop appears in the right thumb and a whorl in the left, the sequence is:

$$\frac{S}{I} \quad \frac{M}{I} \quad \frac{L}{I} \quad \frac{S}{M} \quad \frac{M}{M} \quad \frac{L}{M} \quad \frac{S}{O} \quad \frac{M}{O} \quad \frac{L}{O}$$

VII. Second Sub-Secondary

$$\frac{SSS}{SSS} \quad to \quad \frac{LLL}{LLL}$$

The sequence for filing the second sub-secondary is as follows:

$\frac{SSS}{SSS}$	$\frac{SSM}{SSS}$	$\frac{SSL}{SSS}$	$\frac{SMS}{SSS}$	$\frac{SMM}{SSS}$	$\frac{SML}{SSS}$
$\frac{SLS}{SSS}$	$\frac{SLM}{SSS}$	$\frac{SLL}{SSS}$	$\frac{MSS}{SSS}$	$\frac{MSM}{SSS}$	$\frac{MSL}{SSS}$
$\frac{MMS}{SSS}$	$\frac{MMM}{SSS}$	$\frac{MML}{SSS}$	$\frac{MLS}{SSS}$	$\frac{MLM}{SSS}$	$\frac{MLL}{SSS}$
$\frac{LSS}{SSS}$	$\frac{LSM}{SSS}$	$\frac{LSL}{SSS}$	$\frac{LMS}{SSS}$	$\frac{LMM}{SSS}$	$\frac{LML}{SSS}$
$\frac{LLS}{SSS}$	$\frac{LLM}{SSS}$	$\frac{LLL}{SSS}$	*etc., to*		$\frac{LLL}{LLL}$

Each group of numerators becomes in turn the denominator for the complete sequence of numerators listed above.

VI. WCDX Extensions

<u>Codes</u>   <u>Description</u>

W ---------------------- Plain Whorl
C ---------------------- Central Pocket Loop Whorl
D ---------------------- Double Loop Whorl
X ---------------------- Accidental Whorl

$$\frac{W}{W} \quad to \quad \frac{xX3x}{xX3x}$$

The sequence is as follows:

Prints with **c, d, or x** in any finger, other than the index fingers, constitute the small letter group.

W	cWc	xWd	Wdx
cW	cWd	xWx	Wxc
dW	cWx	W2c	Wxd
xW	dWc	Wcd	W2x
Wc	dWd	Wcx	cW2c
Wd	dWx	Wdc	cWcd
Wx	xWc	W2d	cWcx

The sequence proceeds in the same fashion as the *a, t, r,* small-letter sequence.

$$\frac{111}{111} \quad to \quad \frac{777}{777}$$

VII.   Special Loop Extensions used by the F.B.I.

The following is a partial filing sequence for filing this extension:

$\frac{111}{111}$	$\frac{112}{111}$	$\frac{113}{111}$	$\frac{114}{111}$	$\frac{115}{111}$	$\frac{116}{111}$	$\frac{117}{111}$
$\frac{121}{111}$	$\frac{122}{111}$	$\frac{123}{111}$	$\frac{124}{111}$	$\frac{125}{111}$	$\frac{126}{111}$	$\frac{127}{111}$
$\frac{131}{111}$	$\frac{132}{111}$	$\frac{133}{111}$	$\frac{134}{111}$	$\frac{135}{111}$	$\frac{136}{111}$	$\frac{137}{111}$
$\frac{141}{111}$	$\frac{142}{111}$	$\frac{143}{111}$	$\frac{144}{111}$	$\frac{145}{111}$	$\frac{146}{111}$	$\frac{147}{111}$
$\frac{151}{111}$	$\frac{152}{111}$	$\frac{153}{111}$	$\frac{154}{111}$	$\frac{155}{111}$	$\frac{156}{111}$	$\frac{157}{111}$
$\frac{161}{111}$	$\frac{162}{111}$	$\frac{163}{111}$	$\frac{164}{111}$	$\frac{165}{111}$	$\frac{166}{111}$	$\frac{167}{111}$
$\frac{171}{111}$	$\frac{172}{111}$	$\frac{173}{111}$	$\frac{174}{111}$	$\frac{175}{111}$	$\frac{176}{111}$	$\frac{177}{111}$

etc., to $\frac{777}{777}$

VII. Final

No matter how many of these previously described divisions are used, the *final* should sequence each individual group.

The numerical sequence is filed starting from 1. For example, if there are 15 prints in a group having a final of 14, all of these should be filed together and followed by those prints in the same group having a final of 15, etc.

IX. Key

All prints appearing in a designated final group are arranged by the key in numerical sequence starting from 1. For example, if there are five prints in a group having a key of 14, they should be filed together; followed by those prints in the same group having a key of 15, etc.

Appendix A - Glossary Of Terms

- Two *ridges meeting* (or abutting against each other) is called an **Angle**.

- A Pattern having *two* of the essential characters of a loop, but lacks the third is **_not_** called an **angular type tented arch.**

- On **Arch Patterns** the ridges *enter on one side* of the impression and *flow or tend to flow out the other* with a rise or wave in the center.

- **Bifurcation** - A single ridge *splitting or forking* into two or more branches

- The **Core** is placed *upon* or *within* the *innermost* sufficient recurve.

- The **Core** in a loop pattern is *always upon or within* the innermost sufficient recurve.

- The **Delta** may *not* be *located in the middle of a ridge* running between the type lines toward the core, *but at the nearer end only.*

119

- The **Delta** is placed _on the first recurving ridge_ if there are no ridges between the type lines.

- The **Delta** is that point on a ridge at or in _front of and nearest the center of the divergence_

- **Delta** - That point on a ridge _at or in front of **and** nearest the center of the divergence_ of the pattern area

- A **Delta Ridge** can be joined to - either _one_ or _both_ type lines

- A **Delta** may not be located at a bifurcation - which does _not_ open toward the core

- A **fingerprint** is an impression or reproduction of the friction skin on a surface.

- **Friction Ridge**s (Fingerprint Pattern) remain _unchanged_ during life.

- **Impression** - The **fingerprint pattern** used in classifying

- The _central pocket loop whorl_ will usually have one delta higher than the other. The higher delta is nearer the inner pattern area. The imaginary line between the higher delta and the backside of the innermost recurving ridge is considered the **_inner line of flow_**.

- **Island** (Enclosure) - A single ridge which *forks into two* and *rejoins* into one ridge again

- If the **innermost looping ridge** contains two rods rising as high as the shoulders, *the core is placed upon the end the one farther to the delta.*

- Within a **Loop Pattern** must be *at least one* recurving ridge.

- The requirements of a **Loop** are a *Delta, a Sufficient Recurve, and a Ridge count across a looping ridge.*

- A **Plain Arch** does *not have an upthrust*

- A **Radial Loop** flows *toward* the *thumb.*

- **Recurving ridge** (Also known as a Looping ridge) - A ridge that enters on one side of a finger, curves, and then exits on the *same* side from which it entered.

- The **Ridge Count** of a loop is the *number of ridges crossing or touching an* imaginary line between the delta and the core.

- A *Recurving Ridge* free from any appendages *touching upon the outside of the recurve at a right angle* is a **Sufficient Re-curve.**

- **Tented Arch** - *Angular, up-thrust, and an ending ridge* of any length rising at a sufficient degree from the horizontal plane

- **Type Lines** - The *two innermost ridges* which start parallel, diverge, surround or tend to surround the pattern area

- **Type Lines** are *important to locate the Delta,* but they are from no other significant importance in fingerprint identification.

- **Type Lines** are *not always two* continuous ridges.

- **Up-thrust** is an *ending ridge* of any length rising at a sufficient degree.

- When there is a *choice* **between a bifurcation and another *delta equally* close to the point of divergence - the bifurcation is chosen as the delta**

- When there is a *choice* of **two or more possible Deltas** caused by a series of bifurcations opening toward the core at the point of divergence of the two type lines, *the bifurcation nearest the core is chosen*.

Index

Notes:

Notes:

Made in the USA
Columbia, SC
05 December 2018